BRAVE NEW WORLD
History, Science, and Dystopia

TWAYNE'S MASTERWORK STUDIES
ROBERT LECKER, GENERAL EDITOR

BRAVE NEW WORLD
History, Science, and Dystopia

Robert S. Baker

TWAYNE PUBLISHERS
An Imprint of Simon & Schuster Macmillan
NEW YORK

Prentice Hall International
LONDON · MEXICO CITY · NEW DELHI · SINGAPORE · SYDNEY · TORONTO

Brave New World: History, Science, and Dystopia
Robert S. Baker

Twayne's Masterwork Studies No. 39

Copyright © 1990 by G.K. Hall & Co.
All Rights Reserved
Published by Twayne Publisher
An Imprint of Simon & Schuster Macmillan
1633 Broadway
New York, New York 10019-6785

Copyediting supervised by India Koopman
Book production by Janet Z. Reynolds
Typeset by Huron Valley Graphics, Ann Arbor, Michigan

Printed on permanent/durable acid-free paper
and bound in the Untied States of America

printing number

10 9 8 7 6 5 4 3

Library of Congress Cataloging-in-Publication Data.

Baker, Robert S., 1940–
    Brave new world : history, science, and dystopia / Robert S.
Baker.
        p.   cm.—(Twayne's masterwork studies ; no. 39)
    Bibliography: p.
    Includes index.
    ISBN 0-8057-8077-7 (alk. paper).—ISBN 0-8057-8121-8 (pbk. :
alk. paper)
    1. Huxley, Aldous, 1894–1963. Brave new world. 2. Utopias in
literature. 3. Dystopias in literature. I. Title. II. Series.
PR6015.U9B6725   1990
823'.912—dc20   89-15503
                                                             CIP

Contents

Note on the Text

The text of *Brave New World* used in this study is the Harper and Row edition (1946). This is the most readily available standard edition in the United States, and it offers the additional advantage of identical pagination with the Modern Library edition (1956), published by Random House.

Aldous Huxley.
Photograph courtesy of Matthew Huxley.

Chronology:
Aldous Huxley's Life and Works

1894	Aldous Leonard Huxley born on 26 July, the third son of Leonard Huxley and Julia Francis Arnold.
1908	Enters Eton on a scholarship. Mother dies.
1910	Almost blinded by eye infection. Leaves Eton.
1913	Sight improves. Enters Balliol College, Oxford.
1914	Brother Trev commits suicide.
1915	Joins literary circle of Lady Ottoline Morrell at Garsington Manor House. Meets T. S. Eliot and D. H. Lawrence.
1916	Publishes first volume of poems, *The Burning Wheel*.
1917	Works at the Air Ministry. Teaches at Eton.
1919	Marries Maria Nys, a Belgian war refugee.
1920	Publishes *Limbo*, short stories.
1921	Publishes his first novel, *Crome Yellow*.
1922	Publishes *Mortal Coils*, short stories.
1923	Publishes *Antic Hay*, a novel. Moves to Italy.
1925	Publishes *Those Barren Leaves*, a novel. Begins a world tour.
1926	Publishes *Jesting Pilate*, a travel book. Begins friendship with D. H. Lawrence.
1928	Publishes *Point Counter Point*, a novel.
1929	Publishes *Do What You Will*, first major collection of essays.
1930	Buys house at Sanary in southern France.
1931	Publishes *Music at Night*, essay collection.
1932	Publishes *Brave New World*.
1934	Travels in Mexico and Central America. Publishes *Beyond the Mexique Bay*, essay collection.

1935   Active in H. R. L. Sheppard's Peace Movement, later called Peace Pledge Union. Lectures on peace and disarmament.

1936   Publishes *Eyeless in Gaza*, a novel.

1937   Publishes *Ends and Means*. Moves to southern California. Meets Swami Prabhavananda and joins Vendanta movement.

1939   Publishes *After Many a Summer Dies the Swan*, a novel. Meets Christopher Isherwood.

1941   Publishes *Grey Eminence*, a historical novel. Begins to write scenarios for Hollywood films.

1944   Publishes *Time Must Have a Stop*, a novel.

1945   Publishes *The Perennial Philosophy*, essay collection.

1948   Publishes *Apes and Essence*, a novel.

1950   Publishes *Themes and Variations*, essay collection.

1952   Publishes *The Devils of Loudun*, a historical novel.

1953   Begins to experiment with psychedelic drugs like mescaline.

1954   Publishes *The Doors of Perception*, on drug experiences.

1955   Huxley's wife Maria dies.

1956   Huxley marries Laura Archera.

1958   Publishes *Brave New World Revisited*, a discussion of his earlier dystopia.

1961   Huxley's California home burns; private papers and manuscripts destroyed.

1962   Elected a Companion of Literature of the British Royal Society of Literature. Publishes *Island*, a utopian novel.

1963   Dies in California of cancer, 22 November.

1

Historical Context

Aldous Huxley's most productive period as a novelist spans the two decades most closely identified with literary modernism. A contemporary of James Joyce, T. S. Eliot, and Virginia Woolf, he created his own innovative narrative technique—contrapuntal form—and drew upon many of the current ideas and preoccupations of modernism without ever fully embracing its aesthetic of formal experimentation. In this respect his novels more closely resemble those of Evelyn Waugh, F. Scott Fitzgerald, or Ernest Hemingway, both in their conventional realism and their endeavor to capture the manners and values of the postwar generation. Between 1921 and 1939 Huxley wrote the novels upon which his reputation chiefly rests, satirical narratives in which he sought to define the social milieu of post–World War I England.

His avowed aim was "to write a novel that shall be at once personal and social," in which the central character becomes "a social symbol, a paradigm of the whole life of the community." Such an intention was linked to his interest in history and psychology and his sustained attempt throughout the twenties and thirties to assess the course of postwar history in psychological terms. Such a novel, combining the personal and social in a set of symbolic characters and episodes, he called "the novel of social history."[1] Its most obvious features are scope and an emphasis on ideas; indeed, critics have often attempted to categorize Huxley's work through the term "novel of ideas," although such a phrase is too nebulous and abstract to convey the range and texture of Huxley's characteristic themes.

From *Crome Yellow* (1921) to *Point Counter Point* (1928) and *Eyeless in Gaza* (1936), Huxley focused on the philosophical and social problems of what he saw as an inherently secular society. The point of departure of his social novels is the generational conflict inspired by the Great War. His novels are populated by a younger generation, self-consciously modern, sexually aggressive, and intellectually rebellious. This postwar generation, rendered most vividly in *Antic Hay* (1923), was reacting against an elder Edwardian generation who were regarded as responsible for the most destructive war in history. Huxley's readers were themselves youthful and regarded Huxley as the spokesman of a new and iconoclastic era, bent on repudiating the past but uncertain of the future. In a letter written shortly after its publication, Huxley defended his second novel as "a book written by a member of what I may call the war generation for others of his kind," adding that "it is intended to reflect—fantastically, of course, but none the less faithfully—the life and opinions of an age which has seen the violent disruption of almost all the standards, conventions, and values current in the previous epoch."[2]

Huxley's "novel of social history," then, was aimed at exposing the turmoil of a society aimlessly adrift in the wake of the Great War, animated by a corrosive skepticism yet in search of a framework of moral conviction. Accordingly, his novels are crowded with scientists, artists, historians, and clerics who represented the competing philosophies of the twenties and thirties. Part of Huxley's appeal for his early readers, however, was his refusal to embrace any one philosophy, especially any of the facile notions of historical progress or scientific certitude. The typical Huxleyan hero is usually a shy, introverted figure who lacks a coherent sense of purpose and is lost amid the conflicting ideologies of Marxism, Christianity, liberalism, and fascism.

Historical Context

Searching for human contact, love, or some kind of intellectual stability in a turbulent world, Huxley's heroes contrast vividly with the misguidedly confident apologists for science, art, and religion who surround them and who often take on a grotesquely fanatical form. In the letter quoted above Huxley defended his effort to depict what he called "the life and opinions of an age" but conceded that he had done so in a "fantastical" style. This admission underscores a second major feature of his satirical art. Huxley loved the grotesque; his novels are replete with extravagantly distorted or exaggeratedly abnormal characters. Dwarfs, suicides, sadomasochists, and fanatics of all sorts crowd the pages of *Crome Yellow, Antic Hay,* and *Point Counter Point,* collectively reflecting the social anarchy of postwar Europe.

This medley of conflicting points of view is organized in his narratives in terms of contrapuntal form. The following quotation from *Point Counter Point* is familiar to Huxley's readers as the fullest elaboration of his narrative technique:

> A theme is stated, then developed, pushed out of shape, imperceptibly deformed, until, though still recognizably the same, it has become quite different. In sets of variations the process is carried a step further. Those incredible Diabelli variations, for example. The whole range of thought and feeling, yet all in organic relation to a ridiculous little waltz tune ... All you need is a sufficiency of characters and parallel, contrapuntal plots. ... More interesting, the modulations and variations are also more difficult. A novelist modulates by reduplicating situations and characters. He shows several people falling in love, or dying, or praying in different ways— dissimilars solving the same problem.[3]

Huxley's social novels are organized contrapuntally around repeated episodes and duplicated characters. Such a quasi-musical structure of thematic variation and repetition permitted Huxley to dramatize the shared points of view and the collective trends of a complex social whole. He always regarded society as formidably complex, and consequently his novel of social history customarily registers such "complicated diversities" by means of a large cast of characters who undergo

3

different yet subtly similar experiences and express similar yet significantly divergent opinions. In such a way he sought to reflect what he called the "behavior-patterns, thought-patterns, [and] feeling-patterns" of his contemporaries.[4] Because of his taste for the grotesque, however, the result was more often a discordant cacophony than a harmonious set of musical variations.

One final trait of Huxley's social satire needs to be stressed. As noted earlier, his social novels were, at least in part, rooted in the generational conflict of the 1920s. Their aim of rendering "the whole life of the community" by means of symbolic or paradigmatic characters, fantastical exaggeration, and contrapuntal forms, was shot through with a deep skepticism concerning historical progress and the ends of human history. His attack on an older generation was balanced by his savage criticism of the hedonism of the younger war generation. Moreover his social satire was directed not only at the past and the present but extended to the future as well. Midway through the interwar period (1919–39), he wrote and published *Brave New World* (1932), a futurist novel that, while a radical departure from his more conventional social satire, exemplifies many of its characteristic themes and stylistic traits. Chief among these were his reservations about history, progress, and technology. All of his social novels contain considerable speculation on the direction that technological progress seemed to be taking, on the role of science in modern society, and on the nature of historical process. The search for intellectual certainty and emotional security undertaken by Huxley's heroes takes place in a world recently awakened to the violence of history, a world shaped by the scientific advances of the nineteenth century, by the intense industrialization of the twentieth, and by the advances in technology that were rapidly altering the fabric of British society. Such accelerated progress was a challenge to traditional religion and political ideology, especially in a society shaken by world war and the Russian revolution.

Huxley attempted to capture and assess this intellectual and social turmoil as a kind of psychological historian. One of the persistent assumptions in his writings of the twenties and thirties was his belief that society and history could be interpreted from the perspective of the psychologist. Such a belief was a commonplace among Huxley's contemporaries, writers like Stephen Spender, W. H. Auden, and Raymond Postgate, who thought that social processes and historical change could be comprehended by means of psychological categories. This hypothesis was always vaguely conceived, a suggestive but somewhat nebulous aspiration rather than a cogently formulated theory. For example, Huxley extensively utilized Freudian psychoanalytic concepts in his novels, yet he remained highly critical of Freud in his essays and nonfiction works. In many of his novels, including *Brave New World,* he dramatized his characters in terms of oedipal fixations, sadomasochistic behavior, and broadly neurotic tendencies in order to illustrate what he saw as the general "behavior-patterns" of his contemporaries. In *Brave New World* he drew upon behaviorist psychology as well as Freudian psychoanalytic ideas in a manner that closely conforms to his practice in more conventional novels like *Those Barren Leaves* or *Point Counter Point.* In these works his use of psychological abnormality and, especially, neurotically self-destructive behavior was satirical to the extent that it offered Huxley a means of dramatically rendering what in *Point Counter Point* he called "the disease of modern man."[5]

Like so many of his contemporaries Huxley regarded English—or for that matter, European—culture as having entered a period of decline. His satirical novels are animated by a sense of crisis, social disintegration, and imminent collapse. Deploying an imagery of regression, degeneracy, and inward decay, his work, like that of D. H. Lawrence and Evelyn Waugh, repudiated modern theories of historical progress. In 1931, the year prior to the publication of *Brave New World,* he complained, "It's a bad world; at the moment worse than usual. One has the impression of being in a lunatic asylum—at the mercy of drivelling imbeciles and dangerous madmen in a state of frenzy—the politicians."[6] *Brave New World* is a projection of such fears into the distant future of a scientifically conceived utopia. It was influenced by similar utopian and anti-utopian novels by H. G. Wells and Eugene Zamiatin, but in its stress on economics, psychology, science, and radical social change it is very much a product of Huxley's endeavor throughout the interwar period to write "the novel of social history." In this respect it is a serious political novel as well as an amusing futurist fantasy and has taken its place as one of the major instances of modern dystopian fiction.

2

The Importance of the Work

Within the chaotic disruptions of modern history the philosopher and social historian Theodor Adorno professed to see a single thread or pattern of continuity, the rise of science and, in particular, the increasing power of technology. Adorno, although he admired the achievements of modern science, feared its ability to manipulate, control, and master nature. What he especially feared was instrumental reason, the human capacity to reduce natural processes to merely instrumental status. The historical result was, he claimed, a progressive refinement of technology that, proceeding first to "the control of nature" and then "progressing to rule over men," would finally culminate in a technocracy that would rule "over men's inner nature." He then added, "No universal history leads from savagery to humanitarianism, but there is one leading from the slingshot to the megaton bomb."[7] Aldous Huxley shared Adorno's doubts about the social effects of modern technology. In a letter to E. M. Forster, written in 1935, only three years after the appearance of *Brave New World,* Huxley recorded a conversation with Bertrand Russell in which Russell attempted to discern a ray of scientific light at the end of a historical tunnel darkened by the Great Depression, the rise of Adolf Hitler, and the increasing prospects of war in Europe and Asia: "Bertie Russell, whom I've just been lunching with, says one oughtn't to mind about the superficial things like ideas, manners, politics, even wars—that the really important things, conditioned by scientific technique, go steadily on and up . . . in a straight, unundulating trajectory." Huxley observed that "it's nice to think so" but wondered "if that straight trajectory isn't aiming directly for some fantastic denial of humanity."[8]

In *Brave New World* Huxley had already depicted one major form that such a denial of humanity could take and in doing so created an anti-utopian satire that has only gained in relevance over the intervening years. The reason for this lies with Huxley's decision to focus not simply on totalitarian politics in his vision of a future world state but specifically on the power impulse within science itself. Born into a family with traditional ties to science, Huxley respected scientists and regarded modern scientific methodology as one of the most significant achievements in human history. But he also viewed science, especially applied science or technology, as a powerful expression of darker forces as well as potentially enlightening ones. He feared that the combination of bureaucracy and technology would lead to the rise of a managerial class of technical specialists who valued order and security above all else. In short, he feared the rise of the technocrat and what Christopher Lasch has called "the shift from an authoritative to a therapeutic mode of social control."[9] What especially fascinated him was genetic engineering and its potential capacity to completely transform human society, politics, and even the family.

What makes *Brave New World* such an unusually lasting work, still capable of addressing a contemporary audience with point and vigor, is at least in part attributable to Huxley's decision to concentrate on three interrelated themes: the rise of a society organized around mass consumption; the increasingly ominous developments in the field of genetics; and the political dangers posed—potentially—by the scientific specialist, particularly when organized and empowered by bureaucracy. The most menacing of these, as well as the most vividly and explicitly dramatized in *Brave New World,* is the complex mingling of benefit and political evil that Huxley saw in genetic engineering.

Recently the National Academy of Sciences proposed a three billion dollar project to determine the complete chemical data base of human genes. Cattle have been cloned on Texas farms where patented genetically improved animals are regarded as the economic property of their "inventors." The ability to identify and locate the gene responsible for a particular inherited quality is no longer a scientific fantasy. The technique of cloning, that is, of creating virtually identical organisms by means of exchanging the nuclei of cells that contain genetic instructions, is a proven breeding method, while the Supreme Court of the United States has approved the making of genetically altered bacteria. The alteration of human beings, indeed the creation of genetically designed types for specific tasks, is a complicated moral and philosophical issue as well as a technical one. Most recently, British scientists have claimed to identify the gene responsible for schizophrenia. The idea that there is a direct link between a gene and complex behavior is no longer a highly speculative notion. The implications of this for our notions of individuality, free will, legal responsibility, and even racial and gender identity are only barely understood. Experimental advances in genetic engineering are outpacing our ability to prepare for their ethical and political consequences. If a gene is responsible for our sense of who and what we are, and if a gene can be altered or exchanged, then the personal attributes that compose our sense of irreducible selfhood can be radically modified, even obliterated. How do we utilize such awesome knowledge? Will we relinquish personal and legal autonomy? Who will be empowered by such knowledge?

Huxley's *Brave New World* is an attempt to trace out the darker lineaments of a science that promises a world of altered, cloned, and patented organisms. The problem for Huxley—and for us—is not genetics or science per se, but the potential exploitation of technological advances by a society given over to rampant consumerism, governed by massive centralized bureaucracy, and submissive to the ministrations of the expert or specialist. The twentieth century has seen so many scientific ideas appropriated by governmental bureaucracies for humanly and environmentally destructive purposes that it is hard not to assume that some bitter lessons may be in store for us once the genetic genie is out of the test tube.

Brave New World, however, is not reducible to a dark prophecy of the social implications of genetic research. It is also a study of a culture that has surrendered to mass consumption to the extent that its inhabitants are consumers, even commodities, but never citizens. It is a study of mass culture and industrial technology in a world state where economic and social stability compensates for the vulgarization of intellectual life and the absence of political responsibility. Its presiding feature is the dilution of high culture by means of mass media and popular entertainment. The infantile hedonism of its population and their cynical manipulation by a managerial elite is not as alien a vision as one might wish as the twentieth century draws to its close. Huxley's anti-utopia, then, is both a social and a political novel. The issues that it raises are as exigent and appropriate for 1989 as they were for 1932, perhaps even more so as a result of the even greater complexity of late twentieth century society and its extraordinary advances in technology.

3

Critical Reception

The publication in 1932 of Aldous Huxley's *Brave New World* was greeted with reviews ranging from confused resentment, even outright hostility, to high acclaim. Selling thirteen thousand copies in 1932 (a respectable figure at the time) and ten thousand in the following year, it was eventually translated into nineteen languages and continues to sell at a substantial rate. Initially its most positive reviews were those of scientists like Joseph Needham, who believed that possibly "only biologists and philosophers will really appreciate the full force of Mr. Huxley's remarkable book."[10] H. G. Wells, on the other hand, wrote Huxley a letter in which he accused him of "treason to science and defeatist pessimism,"[11] an attitude shared by Wyndham Lewis, who stigmatized the novel as "an unforgivable offence to Progress."[12] Some of the reviewers simply dismissed the book as a thinly conceived joke or heavy-handed propaganda, unable or unwilling to comprehend the seriousness of Huxley's satire, and going so far as to speculate on whether he approved of his vision of a technocratic future. In the midst of this chorus of bewildered resentment, Rebecca West's *Daily Telegraph* review for 5 February 1932 stands out with clarity and point. Praising *Brave New World* as a work "of major importance," she noted that "the society which Mr. Huxley represents as being founded on this basis [genetic engineering] is actually the kind of society that various living people, notably in America and Russia, and in connection with the Bolshevist and Behaviorist movements, have expressed a desire to establish." Her emphasis on the political implications of Huxley's satire was acute; she was, moreover, the first to note the resemblance between the final debate in chapter 17 and "The Grand Inquisitor" section of Dostoevsky's *The Brothers Karamazov*. She also recognized the book's humanistic theme, defining it as a sustained attack on a prevailing materialism that had discarded religious and philosophical speculation in favor of a blinkered faith in technology. She concluded her review with high praise: "It is, indeed, almost certainly one of the half-dozen most important books that have been published since the war."[13]

West's extremely flattering assessment of *Brave New World* was reinforced three months later by Joseph Needham's May 1932 review in *Scrutiny*. Needham was an internationally known scientist, one of the leading biochemists of his day, and the endorsement of such an acclaimed expert was significant.

> In the world at large, those persons, and there will be many, who do not approve of his "utopia," will say, we can't believe all this, the biology is all wrong, it couldn't happen. Unfortunately, what gives the biologist a sardonic smile as he reads it, is the fact that *the biology is perfectly right*, and Mr. Huxley has included nothing in his book but what might be regarded as legitimate extrapolations from knowledge and power that we already have. Successful experiments are even now being made in the cultivation of embryos of small mammals in vitro, and one of the most horrible of Mr. Huxley's predictions, the production of numerous low-grade workers of precisely identical genetic constitution from one egg, is perfectly possible.[14]

J. B. S. Haldane made much the same claim thirty years later in *Man and His Future* (1963), and Gordon Rattray Taylor in *The Biological Time-Bomb* (1969) more than echoed Haldane when he prophesied that "Brave New World is on its way."[15]

Critical Reception

Many readers, however, were more troubled by the political and religious dimensions of Huxley's narrative, their objections centering on the character of John, a young man brought up on a Savage Reservation. Gerald Bullett complained in the *Fortnightly Review* of March 1932 that, through John, Huxley was promoting the puritanical view that "physical pain is good for the soul" and that "discomfort is a holier state than comfort." Bullett saw the novel solely in religious terms and accused Huxley of being an "angry puritan" who would soon "be received, with loud applause from the faithful, into the bosom of the Church of Rome."[16] Along the same lines, Charlotte Haldane, the author of her own scientific utopia *Man's World* (1926), praised *Brave New World* in the April 1932 issue of *Nature* as "a very great book" but protested that, with the appearance of John, an antagonism develops within the narrative between Huxley the scientific humanist and Huxley the "masochistic medieval-Christian."[17] Other reviewers also stressed the strain of didacticism ostensibly dominating the latter chapters.

More to the point, critics like George Orwell and Granville Hicks raised the issue of ideology. Orwell, conceding that although *Brave New World* "was a brilliant caricature of the present (the present of 1930), it probably casts no light on the future. No society of that kind would last more than a couple of generations." The reason for the lack of credibility in Huxley's depiction of his ruling class was, Orwell argued, the absence of ideology, of "a strict morality, a quasi-religious belief in itself, a mystique." He also claimed that *Brave New World* demonstrates little "political awareness," focusing instead on "recent biological and psychological theories." Orwell argued—quite mistakenly—that Huxley's World State lacked a clear motivation: "The aim is not economic exploitation, but the desire to bully and dominate does not seem to be a motive either. There is no power hunger, no sadism, no hardness of any kind. Those at the top have no strong motive for staying at the top, and though everyone is happy in a vacuous way, life has become so pointless that it is difficult to believe that such a society could endure."[18] In short, Orwell believed that Huxley did not understand totalitarianism and compared his book unfavorably with Zamiatin's *We*.

The argument over the political status of *Brave New World* continues up to the present. Judith Shklar, in *After Utopia: The Decline of Political Faith* (1957), states flatly that *Brave New World* "is not a picture of a totalitarian state"[19] because it simply equates technology with totalitarianism (although Huxley makes no such connection) and fails to offer any detailed political analysis. Conversely, in the most recent study of Huxley's futurist satire, Peter Firchow argues that if politics can be defined as dealing with "the behavior and organization of men into groups, especially large groups, such as cities or states," then "politics certainly plays a very important role in *Brave New World*."[20]

One of the most interesting of the early reviews is Bertrand Russell's in the *New Leader* of 11 March 1932. Russell, perhaps the greatest British philosopher of the twentieth century, was the author of *The Scientific Outlook*, a study of contemporary science that includes a brief depiction of a scientific utopia that may have influenced Huxley's. Russell's review begins by acknowledging Huxley's "usual masterly skill" in disturbing his readers and then focuses on the political ramifications of the novel. Russell was especially struck by the issue of freedom in relation to the contemporary prospect of war. He took much more seriously the threat posed by the type of technocratic ruling class described in *Brave New World* than Orwell did, seeing it as a real possibility. Russell viewed human history much as Mustapha Mond does in *Brave New World*, that is, as a record of interminable violence and irrationality. With the enormous increase in destructive power of modern military technology, Russell feared that Huxley's World State might well be inevitable:

> If you follow out this thought you will be led straight to Huxley's world as the only civilised world that can be stable. At this stage most people will say: "Then let us have done with civilisation." But that is an abstract thought, not realising in the concrete what such a choice would mean. Are you prepared that ninety-five per cent of

the population should perish by poison gases and bacteriological bombs, and that the other five per cent should revert to savagery and live upon the raw fruits of the earth? For this is what will inevitably happen, probably within the next fifty years, unless there is a strong world government. And a strong world government, if brought about by force, will be tyrannical, caring nothing for liberty and aiming primarily at perpetuating its own power. I am afraid, therefore, that, while Mr. Huxley's prophecy is meant to be fantastic, it is all too likely to come true.[21]

Needham believed that the biology of *Brave New World* was "perfectly possible"; Russell regarded its coercive governing caste as a political development "all too likely to come true." Yet Orwell insisted that Huxley's anti-utopia was simply not relevant to the ideological conflicts of the twentieth century. Orwell believed that it lacked the compelling authenticity of Zamiatin's *We* because Huxley had cut the ground out from under his feet as a result of his emphasis on a specifically scientific "utopia." In essence Orwell's criticism was directed at the absence of the very possibility of political opposition in Huxley's World State: "In Huxley's book the problem of 'human nature' is in a sense solved, because it assumes that by pre-natal treatment, drugs and hypnotic suggestion the human organism can be specialised in any way that is desired. A first-rate scientific worker is as easily produced as an Epsilon semi-moron, and in either case the vestiges of primitive instincts, such as maternal feeling or the desire for liberty, are easily dealt with."[22] That last phrase is the crux of the problem for Orwell. How can a race of either moronic zombies or psychologically determined intellectuals do anything but consent to the authority of the state? Orwell underestimated the monolithic power of Huxley's "utopian" state, just as he missed its sadistic overtones (he claimed the novel contained "no sadism" when, in fact, it is permeated by sadomasochistic acts and impulses).

Yet Orwell's point remains an interesting and provocative one. There is little overt political opposition in *Brave New World* comparable to either Zamiatin's *We* or Orwell's *Nineteen Eighty-Four*. Characters do attempt to resist, but in strangely oblique and uncomprehending ways. The one attempt at self-conscious political opposition, a brief public riot, is quickly suppressed as a result of a psychological incapacity for organized resistance. All of which is to say that the politics of Huxley's novel do not correspond to the ideological realities of the 1930s as Orwell conceived them. Huxley, however, was interested in politics and acutely aware of the problems posed by the rise of both fascist and communist dictatorships and what he called the "ferocious ideologies" of the interwar period. But Orwell never appreciated the subtler political dimension of *Brave New World,* especially as it probed the politics of science.

Brave New World has assumed the status of a classic utopian novel and continues to attract a wide readership and varying critical estimations. Much of the academic response has tended to endorse the earlier assessments of Rebecca West, Joseph Needham, and Bertrand Russell. Yet aspects of the book continue to puzzle. Laurence Brander found that the erotic theme was present merely to sustain the reader's interest: "If any reader flags, he will be sexually titillated."[23] Bernard Crick claimed that "Huxley was satirizing equality: he disliked and feared it, therefore an explicit theme in his satire shows equality through happiness carried too far."[24] Yet the sexual theme cannot be dismissed as merely an attempt to arouse the reader, and, while Huxley was never deeply sympathetic to egalitarian forms of democracy, *Brave New World* is not an attack on equality, at least as Crick defines it.

Nevertheless, many critics and readers have been troubled by Huxley's carefully qualified elitism, or what he referred to as "pessimistic humanism," particularly as it manifested itself in the context of sexual relations. The German novelist Thomas Mann, who found in Huxley's work "a splendid expression of the West European spirit," was also disturbed by what he believed to be Huxley's "hate of all fleshly life."[25] Gerald Bullett's review of *Brave New World* accused Huxley of "contempt" for "ordinary human nature."[26] Alternatively, Hermann Hesse's review saw no disgust with human nature, only "melancholy irony" in Huxley's depiction of a mechanized "utopia" where "the human beings themselves have long since ceased to be

human but are only 'standardized' machines."[27] The British novelist
C. P. Snow, writing in the *Cambridge Review* of 17 February 1933,
praised Huxley for having "the response to the sensuous world which
has been bred in every major novelist since Proust." Snow, who regarded Huxley as "the most significant English novelist of his day,"
was especially struck by his "emotional sensitivity,"[28] praise that elic-
ited a sharp rejoinder from Elizabeth Downs. Conceding what she
described as "his masterly and effective satire," she defined Huxley's
art as "the art of exposure, not of creation" because of his "brutal
dislike and contempt of the very limited range of characters he pres-
ents."[29] D. H. Lawrence, a close friend of Huxley's, had complained
earlier of the pervasiveness of "murder, suicide, and rape" in Huxley's
satire,[30] while Arnold Bennett, commenting on *Point Counter Point,*
confessed to enjoying the "tonic brutality" of the book but, nevertheless, charged that "the author gives the impression that he hates and
despises his characters."[31] This kind of attack has dogged Huxley's
reputation up to the present: it is often exaggerated and rooted in the
reviewer's own prejudices and misconceptions about Huxley's satiric
texts. More recently Jerome Meckier has argued that, though Huxley
was "at times, one suspects, abnormally adverse to the physical side of
man," his "anti-physical satire often serves as a forceful satiric
weapon, and is always a complement to his anti-intellectual satire,
both satires stemming from dedication to the ideal of balance."[32]

Brave New World is now generally regarded as one of the classic
texts in the development of utopian fiction, notable, in Philip Thody's
view, for "its concision, social relevance, dramatic qualities, scientific
ingenuity and technical expertise."[33] As Cyril Connolly observed
thirty years after its appearance, "to write a philosophic, even a didac-
tic novel about an imaginary Utopia is a most difficult thing. Too often
the characters in Utopias are unreal while their opinions are cloaked in
the dust of the lecture room. *Brave New World* is an exception because of the ferocious energy of the satire."[34] It was, at least in part,
the ferocity of Huxley's satiric thrusts against his contemporaries'
fascination with Freudian, Marxist, or scientific ideas that energized
his novels, endowing them with both analytic complexity and, on

occasion, a morbidity of tone. But he remained, throughout the twenties and thirties, in the words of one of his contemporaries, George Woodcock, a "historian of attitudes" whose liberal skepticism and trenchant social criticism stimulated a generation: "The point I would make is that at the end of the Thirties, despite the rival attractions of fashionable Marxism, a great many young people regarded Huxley not only as one of the finest novelists of the time, but also as a prophet who in many ways spoke on their behalf."[35]

A READING

Part 1
The Boundaries of Utopia

4

The Modern Utopia: Huxley and H. G. Wells

In *Nineteen Eighty-Four* George Orwell observed that "in the early twentieth century, the vision of a future society unbelievably rich, leisured, orderly, and efficient—a glittering antiseptic world of glass and steel and snow-white concrete—was part of the consciousness of nearly every literate person. Science and technology were developing at a prodigious speed, and it seemed natural to assume that they would go on developing."[36] Aldous Huxley's *Brave New World,* published in 1932, seventeen years before the appearance of Orwell's novel, was aimed at such an optimistic vision of a gleaming technocracy, and like most dystopias or, to use Huxley's term, negative utopias, it expressed the forebodings and anxieties of a generation. The early reviewers were quick to seize upon this dimension of Huxley's novel, Rebecca West praising it in the *Daily Telegraph* as "one of the half-dozen most important books that have been published since the war." While West read it as "equally a denunciation of Capitalism and Communism,"[37] the biochemist Joseph Needham applauded its scientific accuracy, characterizing its biological ideas as especially vivid "patches of shining colour like man-eating orchids in a tropical forest."[38] For Needham,

Huxley's scientific jungle was a very real possibility, a judgment shared by Huxley himself.

The dystopia of the first half of the twentieth century drew on topical events, anchoring its vision of a nightmarish future in contemporary fears of totalitarian ideology and uncontrolled advances in technology and science. As political satire the modern dystopia placed in the foreground concerns and anxieties that were often relegated to the backgound in conventional fiction. It attempted to make explicit the ideological and social ramifications of a too-optimistic interpretation of historical progress, including the hegemonic institutions that might accompany such a misplaced faith in human perfectibility. In doing so, it focused inevitably on the relationship between the individual and the state, on the increasingly apparent danger of social regimentation within an overorganized society, and on the sources of state power in science, technology, and the mass media. If the utopia was a glittering vision of a paradisiacal future, its opposite, the dystopia, was a totalitarian blueprint.

In a letter to George Orwell written shortly after the publication of *Nineteen Eighty-Four,* Huxley praised Orwell's novel as a "profoundly important" work but raised specific objections to Orwell's treatment of what Huxley called "the ultimate revolution." Such a final transformation of society, he argued, "lies beyond politics and economics, and . . . aims at the total subversion of the individual's psychology and physiology." Huxley's use of "politics" here should not be viewed as in any way dismissive. *Brave New World* involves political acts and values as well as economic motives and forces. However, Huxley doubted whether what Orwell called "the policy of the boot-on-the-face" of conventional totalitarian practice could "go on indefinitely. . . . My own belief is that the ruling oligarchy will find less arduous and wasteful ways of governing and of satisfying its lust for power, and that these ways will resemble those which I described in *Brave New World.*"[39] The comparison of Huxley's World State with Orwell's more sadistically oppressive Oceania was inevitable and has continued up to the present to engender much critical chase and scurry. Huxley believed his own futurist satire to be the more prophetic, and he identified his essential theme as the desire for political power by a small oligarchy who achieve their ends by means of subtler, more scientifically based methods than the members of Orwell's "inner party." Unable to resist a final judgment, Huxley concluded his letter with the observation that "the lust for power can be just as completely satisfied by suggesting people into loving their servitude as by flogging and kicking them into obedience. In other words, I feel that the nightmare of *Nineteen Eighty-Four* is destined to modulate into the nightmare of a world having more resemblance to that which I imagined in *Brave New World*."[40]

Huxley denies us a choice of nightmare because of his own philosophy of history; in particular, his conviction that in 1932 he was living in an age in which science had outstripped ethics, and in which there was "every reason to suppose that the world will become even more completely technicized, even more elaborately regimented, than it is at present."[41] Orwell, in 1949, had the experiences of the decade of the 1930s—the rise to power of Adolf Hitler, the Spanish civil war, the Stalinist show trials and purges—and, finally, the Second World War and the collapse of the Yalta accords, to shape his interpretation of modern history. *Brave New World* is also concerned with the course of twentieth-century history and the political ideologies of Europe and America after the First World War, but Huxley, even in 1949, seventeen years after the publication of *Brave New World*, believed his dystopian nightmare to be the more authentically symptomatic of what, in *Point Counter Point*, he called "the disease of modern man."

In May of 1931 Huxley informed a friend that he was "writing a novel about the future—on the horror of the Wellsian Utopia and a revolt against it."[42] The utopian novels of H. G. Wells, particularly *A Modern Utopia* (1905) and *Men Like Gods* (1923), went far to establish the generic features of the twentieth-century utopian narrative. Viewed as a genre or classifiable literary type, the novel in its broadest sense is, as Mikhail Bakhtin has argued, an inherently unfixed form the open-endedness of which defies categorization. It is admittedly difficult to decide just what features shared by, say, *Tristram Shandy*, *Jane Eyre*, and *To the Lighthouse* would collectively constitute that hybrid entity we call a novel. But in its more popular forms (detective fiction, espionage novels, westerns, science fiction, etc.) narrative tends to adopt more predictably specifiable conventions. The classification of literary works according to their formal features is a useful exercise to the extent that it assists us in deducing the meaning of the text from its own formulas and conventions. At the same time, we run the risk of engaging in a sterile performance when we view works apart from their historical context and their reception by a specific audience (class, gender, or race). As Huxley's letter suggests, he certainly believed that he knew what a "Wellsian Utopia" was, and he initially conceived of *Brave New World* as a reaction to it. What follows is an attempt to define Huxley's (as well as Orwell's) conception of the Wellsian utopia, because it is against that model, as well as against Zamiatin's *We*, that Huxley's dystopian satire takes on much of its meaning and structure.

As a genre the utopia has a long history, its roots extending back to Plato's *Republic* and St. Augustine's *City of God*. The principal modern example, Sir Thomas More's *Utopia* of 1516, with its Greek title meaning "no place," established the potential of the genre for both the detached depiction of an ideal state and for trenchant satire directed against contemporary cultural and political conditions. From Tommaso Campanella's *The City of the Sun* (1623) and Francis Bacon's *The New Atlantis* (1627) to the highly speculative political writings of Charles Fourier and Pierre Joseph Proudhon, utopian narrative tended to contrast a visionary future with a more sordid present without offering a persuasively detailed explanation of how such a social ideal might be realized. Within the British tradition the utopian romances of Samuel Butler (*Erewhon* 1872) and William Morris (*News from Nowhere* 1891) figure largely, along with the works of H. G. Wells, in the twentieth-century reaction to the utopian narrative and the appearance of its antitype, the dystopia (bad place). As with its optimistic rival, the negative utopia has a long history and can be traced to earlier works like Aristophanes' *The Birds*, Bernard Mandeville's *The Fable of the Bees* (1714), sections of Swift's *Gulliver's Travels* (1726), and Jack London's *Iron Heel* (1907). The defining instance of the modern dystopia, however, is Eugene Zamiatin's *We* (1924), a key text that exercised significant influence on George Orwell's *Nineteen Eighty-Four* (1949) and that went far to establish some of the principal formal characteristics and themes of dystopian fiction, including Huxley's *Brave New World*.

In a 1962 letter to Christopher Collins, Huxley wrote that Wells's *Men Like Gods* "annoyed me to the point of planning a parody, but when I started writing I found the idea of a negative Utopia so interesting that I forgot about Wells and launched into *Brave New World*."[43] But Huxley never forgot Wells, and though his dystopia is by no means merely a parody of *Men Like Gods,* Huxley's fascination with the "idea of a negative Utopia" is deeply rooted in Wells's social-scientific fantasy. Between 1893 and 1945 Wells published well in excess of one hundred books, about half of which involve scientific speculation and fantasy. Among these are a number of utopian narratives that influenced later writers like Zamiatin, Huxley, and Orwell and established the formal conventions of the twentieth-century utopia, inspiring and shaping the later reaction against it. Huxley regarded Wells as a representative figure and observed that "the ideals of an earnest and very intelligent Englishman of the early twentieth century may be studied, in all their process of development, in the long series of Mr. Wells's prophetic books."[44] Wells's utopias compose a synoptic index to the thematic preoccupations and formal characteristics of the modern utopia, ranging in significance from rudimentary technological fantasy to the ideologically complex issues of the politics of utopia. Again, as Huxley insisted: "Our notions of the future have something of that significance which Freud attributes to our dreams. And not our notions of the future only: our notions of the past as well. For if prophecy is an expression of our contemporary fears and wishes, so too, to a very great extent, is history."[45] The Wellsian utopia, then, is a form of prophetic history, rooted in the modes of thought and perception of the age in which it was written.

At the same time, both the utopian and dystopian narrative are speculative forms of history. They purport to describe a set of future developments traceable to present conditions. And while they obviously cannot draw upon demonstrably factual evidence (i.e., the documentary evidence utilized and interpreted by the professional historian), they do claim to describe a political and cultural state of affairs that could conceivably be brought to pass given contemporary events. At the outset, then, it is important to note that the relationship between the utopian narrative and history turns on two distinct yet related critical issues: first, the futurist novel unwittingly but necessarily gives shape to the values, biases, and beliefs of the period in which it was written—a factor to be linked to the perceptible and not-so-perceptible ideology informing the text; and second, the author is confronted with the problem of including within his narrative some account, however brief, of historical process in order to explain the appearance within historical time of his ideal state. In the utopias of Wells, these factors combine with others to create the heady mixture of prophecy, science fantasy, and adventure that made him such a popular proponent of historical progress and technological optimism. While Wells could be naively optimistic in *A Modern Utopia* or *Men Like Gods,* he also wrote dystopian narratives like *The Sleeper Awakes.* His interpretation of the course of human history was never as positively benign as Huxley maintained. The following synthesis of generic traits that together compose the typically Wellsian utopian novel is intended, first, to catalog the affiliated themes and motifs that influenced writers like Huxley and Zamiatin and, second, to identify the various critical problems raised by Wells's vision that led to Huxley's anti-utopian satire.

The Wellsian utopia rests on a significant historical assumption, namely the recognition in the final decades of the nineteenth century that the technological and industrial consequences of modern science were indeed a permanent feature of modern Western culture; in short, the industrial revolution was here to stay, and the urban metropolis was its architectural symbol. The earlier romantic utopia as conceived by poets like Coleridge and Wordsworth that stressed self-sufficient organic communities, oriented toward nature, manual labor, and small-scale production, had been displaced by the exhilarating promises of modern technology and scientific innovation. The Wellsian utopia was an attempt to envision the ideal social state in terms appropriate for a technocratic society, and in doing so it vigorously repudiated the cultural primitivism of Rousseau (a major theme in *Brave New World*). This contrasting of primitive nature and sophisticated technocracy is fundamental to Wells's utopias and to the dystopias of Zamiatin, Huxley, and Orwell. In rejecting the romantic conception of nature as a sphere of innocent spontaneity where the artificial and conventional are seen as distorting interferences with natural processes, Wells was aggressively promoting the new faith in science and instrumental reason. For Wells human affairs are governed by reason and given direction and purpose by scientific method.

The primary trait of the Wellsian utopia lay in its fundamental endorsement of the materialist and scientific promise inherent in the industrial revolution and further evidenced in the rapid acceleration of scientific discovery in the early twentieth century. Nature, either as a moral or aesthetic standard by which human action is measured or as a source of religious or metaphysical insight, is irrelevant to Wells's ideal state. In *Men Like Gods*, Urthred, one of the Utopians, dismisses the notion of nature as personified agency: "These Earthlings do not yet dare to see what our Mother Nature is. At the back of their minds is still the desire to abandon themselves to her. They do not see that except for our eyes and wills, she is purposeless and blind. She is not awful, she is horrible. She takes no heed to our standards, nor to any standards of excellence." Urthred conceives of nature as a dynamic matrix of "continually fluctuating conditions" that must be struggled with and finally dominated: "With Man came Logos, the Word and the Will into our universe."[46] The result of such an unbending endorsement of scientific method on the part of Wells's Utopians was a perception of nature as merely an immense object, a spatiotemporal continuum whose only relationship with humanity was that of knowledge and mastery. Gone were the cultural myths of the noble savage and natural innocence and romatic conceptions of natural modes of perception and intuition. In their place was nature as an object to be known, a source of power to be mastered, and a level of being to be transcended. In Wells's scientific state, to know is inevitably to master.

Men Like Gods is Wells's most representative utopia. Its principal protagonist, Mr. Barnstaple, finds himself accidentally drawn into another dimension as a result of an experiment carried out by a race of Utopians. The Utopians are human beings in a more advanced state of civilization than Mr. Barnstaple or the small party of upper-class English men and women who have accidentally accompanied him into the Utopian dimension. The narrative is simple, consisting chiefly of a series of lectures and conversations between the Utopians and their more primitive English visitors. These often lengthy verbal exchanges are a typical convention of the utopian or dystopian narrative (Huxley, for example, begins *Brave New World* with a lecture). The English visitors, after learning about the social and technological achievements of the Utopians, do, in Wells's view, the typical primitive twentieth-century thing. Unpersuaded by what they see and hear of Utopian morality and culture, they attempt to take it over by force. The more enlightened Barnstaple sides with the Utopians, who swiftly subdue their imperialist guests and transfer them into yet another dimension. Barnstaple is then returned to twentieth-century England, chastened by the irrational violence of his companions but deeply stirred by what he has learned about Utopian science and confirmed in his abiding belief in historical progress and human perfectibility.

Such a plot, while entertainingly comic and occasionally appealing in its adolescent adventures, is principally a vehicle for Wells's historical prophesying and his assessment of the role of science in human culture. The antagonism noted earlier between nature and technocratic humanity is only the first of a series of binary oppositions that inform Wells's utopias. Closely related to the opposition between, on the one hand, primitive nature with its seasonal rhythms and sensual-instinctual manifestations of some more basic level of being and, on the other hand, nature as interpreted by scientific reason and exploited by industrialization and technology is the contrast between utopian and nonutopian forms of government. This leads in turn to a radical distinction between the psychology of the inhabitant of the Wellsian utopia and the state of mind of less-developed humanity. The utopian

The Modern Utopia

and dystopian novel, then, exhibits certain conventional patterns of emplotment whereby a sequence of events is shaped into a narrative or story of a particular kind. Wells's—and, by extension, Huxley's or Zamiatin's—futurist narratives are informed by the following series of binary oppositions. They define the polarities of good and evil in the Wellsian utopia as well as the political or ideological antagonisms that constitute its narrative action. The first column includes the necessary categories that collectively compose the utopian goal toward which the unenlightened but struggling humanity of the second column is ostensibly progressing.

(A) UTOPIAN	(B) NONUTOPIAN
Rationality, logic, instrumental reason	Feeling, emotion, instinct, passion
Nature as spatiotemporal continuum; the known and exploited object of instrumental reason	Primitive Nature; vitalistic, dynamic
World state	Small social groupings
Internationalism	Nationalism
Science	Religion
Community	Individualism
Socialism	Capitalism
Urbanization, architecturally controlled space	Country, forest, uncontrolled space
Ethic of self-renunciation, service, and self-discipline	Ethic of egocentric self-assertion
Limited or no sexuality, state-controlled families, polygamy, eugenics	Sensual pleasure, eroticism, family, monogamous marriage, natural childbirth
Superior modes of communication	Debased language
Classless cooperation, social harmony	Class hierarchy, social conflict

This catalog of thematic oppositions by no means exhausts the polarities informing this genre, but it does include the principal concepts that require discussion and suggests as well the political codings that govern works like *A Modern Utopia* or *Men Like Gods*. Though Wells was never as optimistically naive as Huxley believed, nevertheless, the values of column A are never radically challenged in his utopian or dystopian novels. It is not until the appearance of Zamiatin's *We* and Huxley's *Brave New World* that a majority of the categories in column B are treated as positive and desirable or, at the very least, that the values of column A are challenged, reassessed, or modified.

Wells's Utopians are amazingly cooperative. In *Men Like Gods* they are described as inherently selfless, "a cleaned and perfected humanity" who have found their proper setting in a world described as "practically a communism."[47] They exhibit no conflicts, either within their own minds or in their relationships with others. This absence of either inner conflict or social struggle is linked to their avoidance of strong emotions. They regard passion, especially erotic desire, as irrational, destructive of both mental stability and social harmony. Sexuality is curtailed or nonexistent, and the family is subordinate to the state. Eroticism is always a source of potential disruption for the utopian state, and consequently it must be controlled or challenged in some form by the powers of the state (as it is in very different ways in Haldane's *Man's World*, Huxley's *Brave New World*, and Orwell's *Nineteen Eighty-Four*). In *A Modern Utopia* Wells advocated group marriage of three or more as a means of taming the overheated desires of humanity. In *Men Like Gods* the state assumes responsibility for the education of children and lays down regulations for controlled breeding aimed at the creation of superior physical and psychological types. Utopia and eugenics are inseparable in the works of Wells, Zamiatin, Huxley, and Orwell. Wells's desire to rise above what he once rather lightheartedly referred to as the "simmering hot mud" of human sexuality often took bizarre forms. In *A Modern Utopia* his race of superior males are permitted to engage in sexual intercourse only on days selected by the state. In *The Sleeper Awakes* pleasure cities are created to contain and isolate the sexually incontinent, who eventually waste away without contaminating society with their uncontrollable desires. The potential of uncontrolled gender relationships, including both those centering on erotic pleasure and those involving childbearing, to destabilize the rational order of utopia is a theme that will recur later in this discussion. For now it is sufficient to observe that the heroes of Zamiatin's, Huxley's, and Orwell's attacks on utopian authority are all sexually frustrated males attracted to nonconforming or rebellious females.

The principal characteristic of the Wellsian Utopian, however, and the explanation for the psychological and social placidity of spirit, is his or her absolute devotion to science. In *Men Like Gods* the citizens of Utopia regard science, especially physics and chemistry, not only as a technique of instrumental reason or a body of empirical knowledge, but as a way of life and a state of mind. Science is a mode of perception and being permeating every aspect of their lives; indeed, it is a subsuming activity or a vital energy traceable, according to one of Wells's Utopians, to a basic "curiosity, the play impulse, prolonged and expanded in adult life into an insatiable appetite for knowledge and a habitual creative urgency."[48] That such an appetitive "urgency" could be misdirected, that technological or mechanical power and the desire for control over mind and body could be radically misapplied in dehumanizing ways is never considered in *Men Like Gods* or *A Modern Utopia*.

In Wells's Utopia the ongoing dynamic of creative scientific research assumes the status of a secular religion. Moreover, the supremacy of science and experimental empiricism is, for Wells, the best possible evidence of historical progress. In the "scientific state" of *Men Like Gods*, the research laboratory is the culminating terminus to history. Such an unquestioning endorsement of rationalism and scientific method finds its complement in Wells's politics and his interpretation of history—at least, as evolved in his utopian novels and books.

Wells's ideal states, however, are only in part a product of a gradualist theory of historical progress, a theory that regards men and women as slowly and indefinitely advancing in a desirable direction as determined by the psychological and social nature of humanity. In the

Wellsian utopian narrative the ideal utopia dramatically emerges as the result of a catastrophic series of events. (Zamiatin, Huxley, and Orwell also provide their novels with similar chronicles of earlier history.) In Wells's *Men Like Gods,* Urthred narrates the history of Utopia in a manner that lies at the basis of Huxley's antagonism to the Wellsian form of this genre.

The world state is described as the result of a chaotic process of social, economic, and political disintegration. According to Urthred, the civilization of Utopia was preceded by "the Last Age of Confusion," a violent period of planetary war, financial collapse, and various civil conflicts followed by unsuccessful attempts at social revolution. Overpopulation and, especially, capitalist economics are stressed as the principal causes of social collapse. Indeed, Wells's Utopia is founded on an explicit repudiation of capitalism. Urthred attributes the instability of the Age of Confusion to the exploitation of the impoverished many by "the predatory and acquisitive few." History is a dark record of increasing economic instability, of domination and oppression in which the idea of competition espoused by laissez-faire capitalists, men who "came to power through floundering business enterprises and financial cunning," not only undermines the civil fabric of organized society but corrupts science as well. Urthred notes bitterly that "adventurers of finance and speculative business" supplanted "pure science" by a thoroughly "commercialized" version leading to a further deterioration into "a new series of Dark Ages."[49] Surprisingly, such a gloomy assessment of human prospects is given a sudden positive twist. Urthred observes that at some undetermined point in history a change occurred in human thinking in which "the old conception of social life in the state, as a limited and legalized struggle of men and women to get the better of one another, was becoming too dangerous to endure." The presumably controlled aggression of capitalist economic competition had become menacingly uncontrolled, while nationalism and a universal arms race demanded some form of international organization. The underlying cause is described by Urthred as a form of social Darwinism, a state of social anarchy energized by "the primordial fierce combativeness of the ancestral man-ape."[50]

Again, nature, in this case the ostensibly natural origins of humanity, is condemned as the source of human irrationality. According to
Urthred, "there had to be new ideas and new conventions of human
association if history was not to end in disaster and collapse."[51] Up to
this point Wells has, through Urthred's narrative, plotted human history as a tragic story in which the hero (humanity) falls as the result of
a fundamental natural flaw, in this case, the primitive aggressiveness
natural to men and women. But suddenly and unaccountably Urthred
transforms his historical tragedy into a drama of redemption, albeit a
confused one. He simply claims that the old ideology of capitalism and
self-assertive egoism disappeared. It had been replaced by "the idea of
creative service" and an ethic of self-renunciation. This alteration in
human consciousness was not the result of a violent revolution but
rather of the extended labors of an intellectual elite, a professional
minority of "inquirers and workers." These disinterested researchers,
"brought into unconscious cooperation by a common impulse to service and common lucidity and veracity of mind," laid the basis for a
sweeping social transformation, "not one of those violent changes
which our world has learned to call revolutions, but an increase of
light, a dawn of new ideas, in which the things of the old order went
on for a time with diminishing vigour until people began as a matter of
common sense to do the new things in the place of the old."[52] Such a
sweepingly optimistic assessment of human potential, coming on the
heels of Urthred's evocation of the excesses and disasters of the Age of
Confusion, seemed to Huxley unconvincing, if not ludicrous. The optimistic appeal to "common sense" and the vague, undefined activities
of a professional elite ("the beginnings of the new order were in discussions, books, and psychological laboratories; the soil in which it grew
was found in schools and colleges") and, finally, the belief in the
possibility of "unconscious cooperation by a common impulse" doubt-
less irritated Huxley, as he noted in his letter to Collins. Wells's Utopia, as historically evoked by Urthred, was, in Huxley's view, a fantasy
of human perfectibility. It assumed both a crippling primitiveness in
human nature and the ability to overcome that primordial egotism on
the basis of an assumed rationality forced into predominance as the

result of the desperate exigencies of history. After five centuries of struggle against exploitative capitalism in which a million deaths occurred, Utopia, we are told, simply came into being: "No date could be fixed for the change," says Urthred. "A time came when Utopia perceived that it was day and that a new order of things had replaced the old."[53]

Wells's Utopia, then, is a fundamentally socialist state, "practically a communism." Private property has been almost totally banished, capitalist free market economics suppressed, "rentier classes" (i.e., those who profit indirectly through investments, rents, and interest) abolished and, along with them, class divisions. Population has been limited by means of a comprehensive program of state-sponsored birth control. The Utopian state itself is conceived as a free association of men and women, who, as a consequence of their enlightened education, voluntarily submit to the guidance of experts. Within such a cooperative meritocracy there are no institutions and no recognizable governmental or administrative infrastructure. The last politician in Utopia, Barnstaple is informed, died a thousand years earlier. More ominous, however, is the absence of defective individuals, all of whom have been bred out of the race; this includes not only those of inferior intelligence but those with weak imaginations, lethargic tendencies, even those susceptible to melancholia or depression. As one of Wells's Utopians rather disturbingly boasts: "Utopia has no parliament, no politics, no private wealth, no business competition, no police nor prisons, no lunatics, no defectives nor cripples."[54]

Wells's "scientific state" rests not on a foundation of governmental agency but on a shared state of mind best exemplified in the Utopian motto: "*Our education is our government.*" Such a state is a perplexing fusion of liberal, progressivist, socialist, Marxist, and even anarchist notions that Wells specifically disassociates from Marxist-Leninist ideology, or what he customarily refers to as "Bolshevism." At the conclusion of *Men Like Gods* he observes that twentieth-century humanity has the germs of Utopia within it, the main evidence being socialism's struggle not only with "the lie of monarchy, the lies of dogmatic religion and dogmatic morality" but especially with the specter of "Bolshevik" ideology and its presence within "the narrowness of the Marxist formula."[55] Wells opposes Marxism and capitalism with his own ideology of science. The scientific state created by the Utopian reformers exemplifies what they refer to as the five principles of Utopia: privacy, free movement, honesty, free discussion or criticism, and unlimited knowledge. What is particularly revealing about this deliberately constricted list of vaguely liberal values is that it is too incomplete to function as a political philosophy. Rather, it stresses just those principles and beliefs necessary to the productive functioning of scientific research. The educational state is in essence a vast laboratory, energized by an insatiable appetite for information, dedicated to the discovery of "new powers," and intoxicated by the possibility of overcoming the "limitations" of time and space. The motivating vision of such a state is the mastery of nature through the intervention of instrumental reason.

In his later novels Wells was not oblivious to the more sinister potentialities of science, but in *A Modern Utopia* and *Men Like Gods* he never satisfactorily disposed of the two critical questions that would preoccupy Huxley in *Brave New World* or Bertrand Russell in his version of a scientific utopia in *The Scientific Outlook:* first, the problem of the ideology of science (i.e., the problem of human ambition and the desire for power, not only in the sociopolitical and individual psychological spheres, but also as it informs science itself) and second, the relationship between scientific rationalism and nature, including the integration within the individual psyche of reason and emotion, rational mind and instinctual desire. In *Men Like Gods* Wells's answer is simply that Utopian humanity, after centuries of suffering, sensibly submitted to the principle of civic service and devoted itself to rational self-discipline and scientific advancement within an elitist, socialist setting.

5

The Modern Dystopia:
Huxley, H. G. Wells, and Eugene Zamiatin

Huxley described *Brave New World* as a negative utopia, that is, a genre best defined as a literary inversion of the principal conventions of its Wellsian opposite. As a mirror image of the utopian narrative it inverts the generic features of a work like *Men Like Gods,* representing them, so to speak, through a glass darkly, not so much to displace the sunny features of Wells's scientific paradise as to bring out what is already there concealed in the shadows or implied in its more sinister, darker lineaments. The generic conventions of the Wellsian utopia listed under column A in the chart in chapter 4 can be viewed as the inverted reflection of the nonutopian categories of column B. In the dystopias of Zamiatin, Huxley, and Orwell, the features of column B are placed in the foreground as a better alternative to the utopian conventions of column A. In *We* and *Brave New World* the dystopian bad place somewhere ahead of us in the darker contingencies of history is the Wellsian utopia seen in its true light. These nonutopian features inform and shape the dystopian narrative in various ways.

In Wells's dystopia *The Sleeper Awakes* (1899) he attempted to envision a genuinely bad place. Because it is an example of a modern dystopian narrative it is useful to note some of its features before turning to the more substantial dystopia of Eugene Zamiatin. In *The Sleeper Awakes* Wells attempted to conceive of a utopia gone mad, a pathological ancestor of the later *Men Like Gods*. The hero, Graham, after falling into a cataleptic trance lasting for over two centuries, awakens in a world that has evolved into a degenerate parody of utopia. He finds himself in an oppressive world state ruled by an oligarchic Council of capitalists who administer the state's finances. The world state is a gigantic metropolis, a "tyranny of the cities," where wealth is power and where the class system not only survives but is actively nourished. The urban proletariat, known as the Blue Canvas in reference to their coarse workers' clothing, have been systematically reduced to the level of wage slaves by the Labour Department, a degenerate survival of the Salvation Army (Wells was not without a sense of humor). The oligarchic Council that controls the "machine of the city" is opposed by a secret society called the Brotherhood. This faction is led by the labor union leader, Ostrog, who uses its revolutionary, socialist fervor as a front, masking his hidden agenda of promoting a new aristocracy based on Nietzsche's concept of the Overman. The world depicted in *The Sleeper Awakes* is a nightmarish variant of the scientific state of *Men Like Gods* in which the stream of progressive history has been dammed up in a static totalitarian technocracy. One feature of Wells's novel is especially characteristic of the dystopian narrative—the preoccupation with communications media and language. The masses of the Blue Canvas are controlled by an elaborate system of propaganda, including a network of Babble Machines designed to implant "counter suggestions in the cause of law and order."[56] The oppressed workers also speak a debased dialect. This motif of language will recur in the dystopias of Zamiatin, Huxley, and Orwell, only in more complexly subtle forms.

In his attempt to envision a retrogressive future in which science and technology have combined under the auspices of the capitalist financier and the industrial labor organizer to create a world state dedicated to absolute control and domination of its populace, Wells never attacks technology itself. He never suggests that the scientific mentality, in the form of instrumental reason and its desire for mastery and power, might be, if not at the root of the problem, at least a significant part of it. Science, either as a body of knowledge or a methodology, is innocently neutral; consequently, in Wells's dystopia there are no grounds for challenging the utopian categories of column A by means of a reassessment of those of column B. The responsibility for the perversion of utopian ideals lies with the men and women who misemploy the techniques of science or those who financially control the scientific community itself. Between the appearance of *The Island of Doctor Moreau* (1896) and *Mind at the End of Its Tether* (1945), Wells often expressed his fears of the abuse and misemployment of scientific research, a theme that is richly developed in his masterpiece, *Tono-Bungay* (1909). But Wells never deeply sifted and probed the ideology of science; he always assumed its value-free status and, for the most part, attributed its potential subversion to a separate category of explanation such as economics or politics.

The first major variation in the thematic focus and narrative structure of the twentieth-century dystopia was written by the Russian editor of H. G. Wells, Eugene Zamiatin. His major work, *We,* was written in 1920, its first English translation appearing in 1924. Zamiatin took the conventions of the Wellsian utopia and inverted their significance, attacking what Wells praised and defending what Zamiatin evidently believed Wells had misconstrued (i.e., his ideas about nature, sexuality, emotion, etc.). As the editor of a Russian edition of the works of H. G. Wells, Zamiatin admired Wells's humanism and pacifism. As a critic of Wells's ideology of science, he believed that he was extending and developing Wells's social-scientific speculation in a form more appropriate to the political realities of the early twenties. *We,* however, has had a rather troubled literary relationship to its English counterparts. George Orwell has been charged by Isaac Deutscher with extensive borrowing from Zamiatin's text. Deutscher claimed that the principal ideas, characters, imagery, and plot of *Nineteen Eighty-Four* are directly traceable to *We,* while Orwell himself accused Huxley of plagiarizing Zamiatin's novel in much the same way. Huxley's statements as to when or even whether he had read *We* do appear contradictory, suggesting that indeed he may be guilty of an unacknowledged debt to Zamiatin, but the accusations of systematic plagiarism directed against both writers are false.[57] This controversy shows little sign of abatement due to the ambiguous nature of the evidence. A possible explanation, however, for what appears to be unacknowledged borrowing may lie with the narrative codes or characteristic formulas by which a genre projects its particular vision of the world.

The dystopias of Zamiatin, Huxley, and Orwell are responses to, in Fredric Jameson's phrase, "a concrete historical situation," one that includes the rise of totalitarian governments and the increasing power of science and technology. At the same time, their dystopian narratives are shaped and informed by conventions and formulas engendered by the genre's characteristic themes. Mediating between political and cultural history and the literary text, the concept of genre is all-important. Why did certain kinds of narratives, such as utopias, espionage thrillers, mysteries, and science fiction suddenly become popular in the nineteenth century and the first decade of the twentieth? What historical factors conditioned their appearance and popularity? What formal features apparently intrinsic to a genre necessarily appear as features of the text apart from historical considerations? As I noted earlier, Wells's utopian and dystopian novels are structured around a series of thematic polarities that can be traced both to history and to narrative logic. For example, one defining feature of the dystopia is the opposition between scientific culture and primitive nature. The celebration of urban technology and scientific method is a necessary foreground against a background of primitive spontaneity and irrationality. Accordingly, the "primordial man-ape" of *Men Like Gods* reappears in Zamiatin and Huxley, less as a result of literary influence or borrowing than as a consequence of narrative logic. *We, Brave New World,* and *Nineteen Eighty-Four* focus on rigidly controlled technocracies or ostensibly rational scientific states that, on the level of the text, necessarily generate their thematic opposites. Zamiatin's One State is defined by its opposite, the primeval forests that lie beyond the Green Wall. In *Brave New World,* the World State is contrasted to its antitype, the Savage Reservation, while in Orwell's *Nineteen Eighty-*

Four, the totalitarian state of Oceania is juxtaposed with the escape offered by the pastoral countryside, a place of emotional spontaneity and unstructured freedom. These recurrent patterns of opposition do not point to indebtedness or plagiarism, but rather to the formal conventions of the genre.

Eugene Zamiatin's *We* consolidates many of the features of the Wellsian futurist narrative, but it also extends and develops them in more subtle ways. Taking the form of a diary written by a mathematician called D-503, a citizen of the technocratic One State, it records the gradual mental breakdown of its author and his loss of faith in the promises of a scientific utopia. Following the Wellsian pattern, the One State is the product of a period of catastrophic history, including global warfare and economic collapse. Its historical emergence is marked by the appearance of scientific rationality as an all-consuming state of mind within a society dedicated to routine, conformity, and order. The members of this neurotic community, known only by numerals, inhabit a vast city of glass, wear uniforms, and organize their working days according to a rigid schedule. The transparency of the city itself guarantees the absence of privacy and, thus, the eradication of individual, noncommunal space.

In Wells's futurist fantasies, architecture, with its mathematical control of space, is a triumphant expression of instrumental reason and a symbol of the essentially urban future. Always enamored of metropolitan building, Wells created settings of vertiginous heights and depths, vast public spaces organized by domes, arches, and bridges. Surrounded by an architectural ensemble of gleaming towers and monumental masonry, the inhabitant of utopia lived within a symbol of human order and accomplishment. Yet excessively public settings mean that the utopian is also continually subject to the public gaze. Subjected to the symbolism inherent in the vast scale of the urban architectural panorama, dwarfed by its size and subtly influenced by its geometry of ordered spaces, the inhabitant of the metropolis unconsciously responds to its celebration of rationalist achievement and, more dangerously, surrenders to its coercive manipulations. Such a setting of dehumanizing scale, hygienic sterility, and mathematical order is ideology made manifest in concrete and steel. Zamiatin, Huxley, and Orwell were acutely conscious of the political implications of architectural and natural space. In *We* the glass city's transparency symbolizes not an open society but a closed one, where the individual is constrained and bound by social convention and constant political surveillance. Its glass wall dividing the ordered urban spaces from the anarchic, uncontrolled sprawl of nature is repeated with variation by Huxley in *Brave New World* in the form of a great electric fence demarcating the boundary between utopian civilization and the savagery of the New Mexico reservation. But in *We*, the inhabitants beyond the Green Wall manage to overcome the barrier in a brief and ambiguously hopeful revolution that, while it fails, suggests some grounds for future optimism.

Despite the thematic complexity and stylistic subtlety of *We*, the story is formulaic to the extent that it is governed by the narrative codes constraining and informing the dystopia as a genre. The central protagonist, D-503, is in charge of a project to construct and launch a spaceship, the *Integral*. Despite his loyalty to the Benefactor, the totalitarian ruler of the One State, and the watchfulness of the Guardians (the Benefactor's secret police), D-503 meets and falls in love with I-330, the leader of a revolutionary underground called the Mephi (derived from Mephistopheles). Engendering radically new emotions, this sexual encounter with an assertively political woman inaugurates D-503's career of opposition to the Benefactor, especially the latter's project of sending the *Integral* on a mission of spreading the ideology of the One State throughout the universe.

Zamiatin's *We* is the record of D-503's mental collapse into a state of schizophrenia as the two sides of his nature struggle to repress each other. His rational, logical self, loyal to the values of the One State, struggles to subordinate his irrational, instinctual side, symbolized by his lover I-330. It is in fact difficult for the reader to decide whether all or most of the events recorded in the diary have not taken place in the mind of the narrator. This internalization of seemingly external events governs the conclusion of *We* when the authorities of the glass city, aware of growing opposition, initiate a new surgical procedure intended to remove the imagination. After a struggle with the revolutionaries over control of the rocket, D-503 submits to the operation and thus ensures the repression of the irrational forces breaking through the Green Wall. The political uprising is suppressed, and at the conclusion of the narrative the hero serenely watches as his lover, I-330, is tortured to death in the Gas Bell. The final diary entries do, however, state that the revolution of the Mephi is continuing in the outer districts of the city.

Zamiatin's *We* differs from Wells's utopias in that the latter's enthusiasm for not only science but also government consisting solely of the cooperative supervision of scientific experts (like D-503) is subjected to a searching critique. Wells, for example, advocated the state regulation of marriage and sexual experiences. In *Anticipations* he argued that sexual expression should be controlled by the medical doctor and the psychologist, and his governing elite was permitted intercourse one night in five. In *We,* where the citizens of the One State have been carefully trained to regard sexual passion as a wasteful expenditure of energy, Wells's enthusiasm for state intervention in and domination of the private, subjective emotional sphere is satirized as repressive, in both the psychological and political senses. The One State *is* Wells's scientific state in its most potentially dehumanizing form, where simplification, routine, and limitation are the ruling political and intellectual tendencies.

Zamiatin's dystopia is, like Wells's futurist narratives, governed by binary oppositions. The pattern of red and blue imagery that pervades *We* symbolizes the essential antinomies of the narrative and corresponds to column A and B in the chart in chapter 4. Blue symbolizes reason, order, discipline, restraint, mathematics; red is passion, freedom, emotion, spontaneity, energy, nature. Zamiatin repudiates "the dizzying blue"[58] of rationalist idealism fostered by the scientific One State, especially as it endeavors to proscribe and banish the passional interior life of the individual. He is not so much rejecting the values of the Wellsian Utopia of *Men Like Gods* as he is showing how its optimistic reliance on scientific methods and goals could easily degenerate into a world where the interior life is subordinated to the enforced conformities of an excessively rationalized social agenda. The glass city is a society where scientific objectives (within narrowly defined limits) have become the only remaining permissible aspiration. The creative vitality of the human psyche has been systematically subjected to deformative stresses and ultimately to some form of radical annulment (the surgical lobotomy).

In a section of *We* that Huxley may have borrowed from, R-13, the spokesman for the ruling ideology of the One State, informs D-503 that the ancient legend of an Edenic paradise, was, in fact, a prophetic anticipation of the Benefactor's city of glass. In the legend, Adam and Eve had a choice between freedom and happiness: "Just think. Those two, in paradise, were given a choice; happiness without freedom, or freedom without happiness. There was no third alternative. Those idiots chose freedom, and what came of it? Of course, for ages afterward they longed for the chains." Later, when D-503 confronts the Benefactor he is told that the principal desire of humanity is for someone to define absolutely the nature of happiness and then "to bind them to it with a chain."[59] Within the One State, happiness is an absence of self-awareness, a condition of naive unity and harmony in which the citizen is a cooperating cell within a larger organization. The submergence of self-awareness within the social whole requires the rejection of sexual desire or any other assertion of desire productive of inner conflict.

The One State insinuates itself into the nocturnal life of its citizens, forbidding them to remain awake at night, to have unlicensed sexual activity, even to dream. The only permissible outlet for desire is to participate in the cultural struggle toward the ideal of a perfected social order and its unlimited expansion. In Wells's utopias, the utopians' energies are harnessed to the ideal of scientific research and the absolute mastery of nature. In *We*, however, the absolute ideal and the struggle toward its realization is inherently political. The ideal embodied in the rocket, the *Integral,* is not one of scientific exploration or engineering technology, but of expansion into the universe of the One State's ideology of rationalist power. The pure mathematics so cherished by D-503 is the value system of an oppressive rationalism. It functions chiefly as a guarantor of harmonious political order, not as an instrument of innovative research. At the conclusion of *We,* a mathematician of the One State announces that he has proved that infinity does not exist. The world is sharply circumscribed, that is, bounded and limited in a way that conveniently coincides with the nature and ideal of the One State itself.

Zamiatin brilliantly adds to the utopian idiom created by Wells, refining and deploying the latter's thematic categories and stylistic conventions in order to turn them on themselves. In particular, he emphasizes gender relationships that are only tentatively and mutely present in Wells's dystopias like *The Sleeper Awakes.* Just as the appearance of D-503's lover inaugurates his rebellion against the Benefactor, so are the roles of women in *Nineteen Eighty-Four* and, in a somewhat different way, in *Brave New World,* linked to the hero's increasing antagonism to the prevailing political order. It is not until Margaret Atwood's dystopia, *The Handmaid's Tale,* that this thematic convention is fully exploited, although Charlotte Haldane's *Man's World* (1926) develops it in conservative ways. More importantly, Zamiatin begins the exploration of the relationship between knowledge and power that becomes the central theme of the modern dystopia. The access to knowledge and the control of science, not just by business interests or government but by scientists themselves, would become the principal subject of the modern dystopian novel. In each case, however, Zamiatin's innovations are put to related yet subtly different uses in Orwell and Huxley.

If *We* is a dystopic revision of the Wellsian technocratic paradise, attacking its faith in scientific rationality by means of a reassessment of emotion and sensual experience, Huxley's *Brave New World* further develops this conflict between science and nature, or intellect and primitive passional experience, in which one is invariably privileged at the expense of the other. *We,* like Orwell's *Nineteen Eighty-Four,* is among other things the story of a man resuming his humanity, taking political responsibility for his life, and, finally, failing when confronted with the power of the state and his own fearful complicity with it. Its obsessively intricate focus on the individual psyche as the contested battleground over which antagonistic ideologies struggle is a major refinement of the Wellsian futurist novel with its cruder emphasis on external episodes, description, and facile adventure. In its reversal of the thematic oppositions of novels like *A Modern Utopia* and *Men Like Gods*, *We* alters the terms of the debate, calling into question the ideological premises on which the Wellsian futurist novel is based and attempting to rehabilitate the discredited romantic concepts of the creative imagination, cultural primitivism, and nature.

The plot of the anti-utopian novel is generically constrained by the fundamental thematic opposition of freedom and restraint. The characterization of the hero, the structure of the narrative, and the imagery and symbolism of the text are informed and shaped by this central tension between the oppressive organization of the state and the revitalizing anarchy of the individual. Zamiatin's accomplishment was to recognize the political dystopia hidden within Wells's scientific utopia. Huxley, however, would extend this debate by challenging Zamiatin's decision to remain within the categories of opposition defined by Wells. At the risk of oversimplification, it can be said that Wells defined the oppositional categories of the utopian narrative. Zamiatin then revised them. Huxley attempted to transcend them.

6

Historical Progress and the Liberal Dilemma: Utopia and the New Romanticism

One way of approaching the utopian and dystopian narrative is by means of genre, but the classification of literary works according to formal features runs the risk of becoming an empty exercise without the appeal to the reader's expectations within the larger context of history and ideology. Although it is useful to ask what forms, conventions, and narrative formulas inform the modern utopia, such a question is incomplete unless we inquire what meaning and ideologies are peculiar to these conventions and forms. A genre like the utopia projects a specific vision of the world. The modern dystopia, like Zamiatin's *We* or Huxley's *Brave New World,* is as much an expression of contemporary fears and anxieties as it is a further refinement of generic conventions. Huxley consistently maintained that "Wells's prophetic books" were symptomatic of Edwardian ideals and ambitions. Unwilling to halt there, he extended this notion to the writing of history itself, arguing that if social prophecy or speculative fiction is "an expression of our contemporary fears and wishes, so too, to a very great extent, is history."[60] Both the utopian and dystopian novel involve an attempt, first, to envision the end of history or the final terminus of historical development and, second, to describe the totality of social relations as embodied in a single imagined community. Such an aim is, in both cases, inevitably political.

Huxley consistently stressed the degree to which both utopian novels and narrative history were permeated with current prejudices and values. More important, he was justifiably wary of the historical enterprise itself, at least in its broadest manifestations: "Generalized history is a branch of speculation, connected (often rather arbitrarily and uneasily) with certain facts about the past. Circumstances alter, each age must think its own thoughts. Not until there is a settled and definitive world order can there be such a thing as a settled and definitive version of human history."[61] Despite his reservations concerning history, especially speculative history in which an attempt is made in the manner of Hegel or Marx to interpret the entire course of human temporal experience in accordance with some grand design or overarching purpose, Huxley was nevertheless fascinated by history and the time-honored attempt to identify some kind of immanent meaning within the turbulent ebb and flow of historical events. *Brave New World* is, as Huxley said of Wells's utopias, an expression of the fears and hopes of British society of the 1920s and early 1930s as interpreted by a highly educated, upper middle-class author. Despite his reservations about generalized history as a form of dubious speculation, Huxley's dystopia rests on carefully formulated beliefs about politics, history, and society that cannot be fully comprehended apart from contemporary ideas.

In 1929, five years before the publication of *Brave New World,* the socialist writer A. L. Rowse observed that in postwar England "there is no one school of historians which may be said to be predominant; and there is no one conception of history which has been worked out fully or has gained general adhesion."[62] Similarly, in *The Coming Struggle for Power,* published in 1933, the year after the appearance of Huxley's dystopia, the Marxist author John Strachey voiced the presiding anxiety of many of his contemporaries when he asked, "How does history work? How *long* does it take history to work?"[63] In the same year, the economist John Maynard Keynes, hardly a Marxist, was to complain, "We lack more than usual a coherent scheme of progress, a tangible ideal."[64] The search for a tangible ideal based on some notion of how history works was a major preoccupation of most writers of the interwar period. In *The Destructive Element* (1935), the poet and critic Stephen Spender struck a characteristic note when he lamented that contemporary Europe seemed adrift, aimlessly anarchic and bereft of coherent political vision. "The nationalist European state does not provide a sense of historic purposiveness: it does not convince one of its reality. The history of nationalities which we see around us, which we live in, is not a full tide bearing us forward; ours is not an Elizabethan age. On the contrary, the trend of contemporary history, so far from giving us direction, has not even the merit of being obvious. It does not decide our attitude; we have to adopt some analytic attitude towards it."[65] Spender's concern with the apparent aimlessness of contemporary European history was a staple theme of Huxley's satirical novels of the 1920s, including his masterpiece of 1928, *Point Counter Point*. In these novels, beginning with *Crome Yellow* in 1921 and culminating in *After Many a Summer Dies the Swan* of 1938, Huxley attempted to chart the fatalistic drift of English society in the wake of the First World War and to explore the gradual acceleration of historical and social currents within the doctrinaire channels of the ideologies of the 1930s. Like Spender, he was convinced that the modern writer had to adopt "some analytic attitude towards" historical process and the political ideologies animating it.

Stephen Spender was a liberal socialist, influenced by Marx and Freud, and eager to discern in the seemingly random flux of modern history some evidence of design or pattern. Huxley, while not sharing the former's Marxist ideas, was equally struck by the opacity of what Spender called "the trend of contemporary history" and evolved his own explanation of historical trends in the modern period. The interwar period (1919–39) that saw the appearance of Huxley's best work was one of recurrent crisis and fading liberal hopes. The trauma of the Great War, the cultural and political impact of the Russian revolution of 1917, and the rise of European Fascism in Italy had inspired what Huxley called "the ferocious ideologies" of the 1930s. By the late 1920s, dictatorships or strongly authoritarian governments had been established in Italy, Spain, Portugal, Austria, Yugoslavia, Hungary, Poland, and Lithuania. Equally significant was the increasingly widespread tendency to entrust drastic emergency powers to national governments, that is, coalitions composed of all parties but usually dominated by conservatives. In the year before the publication of *Brave New World,* Britain saw the formation of a national government with emergency powers. In the general election of 1931, this coalition, confronted by the economic catastrophe of the Great Depression, asked for a doctor's mandate from the electorate in order to justify its assumption of radical executive and legislative powers. France, under Poincaré, had already experimented with the delegation of special powers to the government, while, in the United States, the authority of President Roosevelt in his New Deal had been extended well beyond the customary powers of his office. In Weimar Germany President Hindenburg was governing on the basis of emergency decrees, while Mussolini and Stalin had consolidated their positions as dictators. Perhaps most significant of all, in the Reichstag elections of 1930 Adolph Hitler's National Socialists had gained their first major electoral victory, and in January of 1933, the year after the publication of *Brave New World,* Hitler became chancellor of Germany.

Certainly the political experiences of Great Britain or France did not match those of Germany and Italy, but the modification or replacement of liberal democratic institutions throughout Europe was a central factor in the period in which *Brave New World* was conceived, written, and published. In his essays of the late twenties Huxley repeatedly noted the degree to which democratic systems of parliamentary government had either broken down or been displaced by authoritarian or dictatorial regimes. In 1927, he observed that "with regard to political democracy, its disadvantages are becoming daily more apparent in America as in all other countries which have adopted it as a system of government," adding with unmistakable sympathy that "a revolt against political democracy has already begun in Europe and is obviously destined to spread."[66] Huxley was not an ardent supporter of republican or parliamentary democracy—at least, not in its early twentieth century forms. Neither was he an advocate for any of the competing ideologies of his contemporaries, including Marxism, communism, or fascism. Rather, he preferred a form of meritocracy, or what he called "the ideal state . . . in which there is a material democracy controlled by an aristocracy of intellect."[67] Huxley's aversion to democratic institutions, especially their populist core, was rooted in a much broader development in European culture throughout the interwar period: the pervasive questioning of liberalism and liberal values.

The failure of liberal politics in the face of the increasing popularity of fascist or communist ideology and its inadequacy to deal effectively with the economic challenges of the Great Depression was regarded by many members of Huxley's generation as symptomatic of a fundamental weakness in liberal philosophy. For example, H. A. L. Fisher, one of the leading English historians of the period, chose for the third volume of his widely acclaimed *A History of Europe* the title *The Liberal Experiment* (1935). For Fisher, the prime source of "evil" in the Europe of the 1920s and 1930s was "the eclipse of Liberalism,"[68] yet as his title suggests, he saw liberalism as an experiment or an insufficiently tested hypothesis that, in October of 1935, was not only still unconcluded, but in very real danger of being prematurely aborted. Fisher's ambitious history is a key test for comprehending the degree to which even a liberal historian of the thirties had come to view the viability of liberal notions of progress and development. Such a political philosophy, stressing individualism, egalitarianism, rationalism, and, especially, a meliorist or progressivist view of human history was, according to Fisher, not only experimental but had, he added, "receded over wide tracts of Europe."[69]

Fisher's history of Europe from the Roman Empire to what he called the tragedy of the Great War is close to what Hayden White in his study of historical narratives would term tragic, and, in this respect, it is characteristic of the intellectual climate of opinion that fostered Huxley's *Brave New World*. Fisher's construal of the pattern of European history from the "common political framework" of Roman civilization to the "novel and unprecedented" condition of twentieth-century Europe was one of increasing fragmentation and division. The last idea expressed in his three-volume history was that of Europe's final destruction, while his synthesis of the general trend of modern European history in his epilogue was informed by a rhetoric of atomization; his favorite words were "cleft," "splintered," "chaos," "rupture," "break-up," and "fracture." History, in Fisher's view, was a cycle of achieved and lost unity, of social calamities, alternating cultural divisions and deepening lines of fracture that culminated in the "tragedy of the Great War and its legacy." He saw Europe on the threshold of a new period of "insane" nationalism and extremist ideologies in which its "moral unity" has been decisively "broken."[70]

This assessment of both the course of European history and its future prospects is important for our comprehension of Huxley's dystopia for two reasons: First, in its passionate, apocalyptic character, it resembles the brief historical narratives characteristic of utopian and dystopian novels; indeed, it could have been spoken by Wells's Urthred in *Men Like Gods* or Huxley's Mustapha Mond in *Brave New World*. Second, Fisher's brief synthesis of European history in terms of "impending historical crisis" is a judgment by one of the leading historians of the 1930s, whose gloomy assessment of liberal theories of historical progress is part of the cultural mood out of which Huxley wrote. Widely read and criticized throughout the period by writers like Stephen Spender, A. L. Rowse, Christopher Caudwell, Leonard Woolf, and E. H. Carr, *The Liberal Experiment* is virtually a synoptic guide to the ideological dilemmas of liberalism in the thirties. It shares with Huxley's essays both the contemporary mood of dampened liberal hope and discrete assumptions about the nature of historical change.

Fisher saw himself as tracing "the general trend of Europe towards nationalism and democracy,"[71] a trend violently disrupted and reversed by the Great War of 1914–18. Huxley too saw the Great War as decisive, and he too conceived of history in terms of collective trends. He rejected the notion espoused by Marxist writers that history could be explained by an appeal to historical laws. In *Proper Studies* (1927), he argued that "the human universe is so enormously complicated that to speak of *the* cause of any event is an absurdity."[72] For Huxley, a historical or sociological fact was part of a tangled causal web, a field of interacting forces so complex that an attempt to isolate simple causal sequences and identify them as historical laws tended to falsify the nature of the events themselves. History, he claimed, "is not a science."[73] Historians who aspired to not only scientific precision in the observation of temporal social events but to the identification of laws governing these events were pursuing an illusion. In *Do What You Will* (1929), he flatly stated that "there is no such thing as Historical Truth—there are only more or less probable opinions about the past, opinions which change from generation to generation."[74]

Huxley's historical and sociological generalizations about the nature of modern history, then, took the form of "probable" opinions concerning "humanly significant"trends, or what he called a "historical undulation." In *The Olive Tree* (1936), he suggested that "history pursues an undulatory course." These all-embracing undulations, he observed, were, in part, the result of a "tendency displayed by human beings to react, after a certain time, away from the prevailing habits of thought and feeling towards other habits." He then added that the "autonomous nature of psychological undulations is confirmed by the facts of history."[75] Huxley believed that collective trends engendered by shared cultural conventions occur throughout history and that they appear as autonomous wholes, that is, as cultural moods, climates of opinion, shared ways of perceiving the world, or philosophical and ideological frameworks. They are intrinsically psychological because they are inspired by emotional and intellectual behavior and, most important, they are attributable to individual actions, not vast impersonal forces. This purposive or individualistic emphasis has important political implications for Huxley's work in that it can be traced to his belief in the relative freedom of "the individual will" and his aversion for deterministic ideologies: "The course of history is undulatory, because (among other reasons) self-conscious men and women easily grow tired of a mode of thought and feeling which has lasted for more than a certain time."[76]

The importance of Huxley's philosphy of history for *Brave New World,* itself a meditation on history, lies in the fact that he believed he had detected the presiding cultural trend of the interwar period: "The activities of our age are uncertain and multifarious. No single literary, artistic, or philosphic tendency predominates. There is a babel of notions and conflicting theories. But in the midst of this general confusion, it is possible to recognize one curious and significant melody, repeated in different keys and by different instruments in every one of the subsidiary babels. It is the tune of our modern romanticism."[77] Huxley defined what he meant by modern romanticism in the years immediately preceding the publication of *Brave New World*. The key essays are contained in two collections, *Proper Studies* (1927) and *Music at Night* (1931), as well as in American periodicals. The pivotal essay is "The New Romanticism" of *Music at Night*.

As the last quoted passage indicates, Huxley saw the intellectual climate of the interwar period as one of indecision and complexity bordering on incoherence. This "multifarious" anarchy of "notions" he traced to a clash of antagonistic ideologies that he termed old and new romanticism. The older version he identified with the poets and philosophers of the romantic period (approximately 1780–1830) or "the romanticism of Shelley, of Victor Hugo, of Beethoven." Such an ideology he saw as inherently liberal, stressing individualism, personal liberty, and an optimistically progressivist view of human history. The following passage is of considerable significance for *Brave New World:*

> It is in the sphere of politics that the difference between the two romanticisms is most immediately apparent. The revolutionaries of a hundred years ago were democrats and individualists. For them the supreme political value was that personal liberty, which Mussolini has described as a putrefying corpse and which the Bolsheviks deride as an ideal invented by and for the leisured bourgeoisie. The men who agitated for the English Reform Bill of 1832, who engineered the Parisian revolution of 1830, were liberals. Individualism and freedom were the ultimate goods which they pursued. The aim of the Communist Revolution in Russia was to deprive the individual of every right, every vestige of personal liberty (including the

liberty of thought and the right to possess a soul), and to transform
him into a component cell of the great 'Collective Man'—that single
mechanical monster who, in the Bolshevik millennium, is to take the
place of the unregimented hordes of 'soul-encumbered' individuals
who now inhabit the earth. . . . To the Bolshevik idealist, Utopia is
indistinguishable from one of Mr. Henry Ford's factories.[78]

The conjuction of liberalism, communism, fascism, and the American
industrial capitalist Henry Ford (the presiding deity of *Brave New
World*) is no accident. The new or modern romanticism was a collectivist ideology, exclusively materialistic and inherently antiliberal. Romanticism, for Huxley, was always associated with ideological extremes, either an excessive endorsement of individualism and personal
freedom (the old or liberal version) or a fanatical belief in technology,
mechanization, and communal or collective experience at the expense
of the individual (the new, antiliberal form). It is important to emphasize that Huxley characterized both positions as "extravagant and
one-sided"; the old romantic liberal refused "to admit that man was a
social animal as well as an individual soul," and the modern romantic
denied "that man is anything more than a social animal, susceptible of
being transformed by proper training into a perfect machine." Huxley
confessed to "no great liking for either of the romanticisms," prefer-
ring the older liberal version only if confronted with the necessity of
choosing it as opposed to materialism or Marxism.[79]

Modern romanticism, then, is an example of what Huxley conceived as a cultural trend. As a form of false utopianism it envisioned
the goal of human history as a collective state, authoritarian and regimented. Its stress on "collective mechanism," despite its fascist and
Marxist formulations, tied it closely to Huxley's perceptions of contemporary European and even American civilization. In "The New
Romanticism" Huxley deliberately links Ford and Lenin in their obsession with industrial technology and mass production. What is particularly significant is the way in which he characterizes modern romanticism as an inherently self-destructive cultural trend, describing it as
"headed straight towards death."[80] The new romanticism embraced

practically everything Huxley rejected in modern English, European, and American culture. He associated it with a deep and life-denying allegiance to collectivist ideologies and their celebrations of technological progress, as well as with a broad spectrum of psychological neurosis and, specifically, sadomasochistic forms of behavior.

This last observation leads to a final and pivotal element within Huxley's assessment of modern history—his belief that history could be cross-indexed with psychology. Huxley construed the processes of modern history in terms of a metaphor of oscillating rhythms of cultural trends that he referred to as "psychological undulations." In *Ends and Means* (1938) he argued that to understand the state and its role in history "we must do so as psychologists" because the events of history "are ultimately psychological in nature." As a result, he claimed, "every culture" was composed of "arbitrary and fortuitous associations of behavior-patterns, thought-patterns, feeling-patterns" that eddy and twist in the larger currents of historical process. Coming together for "long periods" only to succumb to "changing circumstances" and new groupings, these psychological trends like modern romanticism are regarded, so long as they last, as "necessary, natural, right, inherent in the scheme of things."[81] In his satirical novels of the twenties and thirties Huxley attempted to expose and satirize what he saw as the unnecessary, unnatural, and artificially fabricated belief-systems of his contemporaries. In doing so, he stressed aberrant psychological behavior to, at times, an almost morbid degree.

7

Ideology and Power in Huxley's Ultimate Revolution: The Case of the Marquis de Sade

While *ideology* is a somewhat disputed term, there is general agreement on its larger significance. It refers to the collective beliefs of a group, usually a social class, and takes the form of an ostensibly rational and unified interpretation of human goals and aspirations. Although based on a coherently centered system of beliefs about human nature, society, and history, its general thrust is political; indeed, it can be argued that its principal significance lies less with the ideas themselves than with their relationship to the distribution of socioeconomic and political power within society. Aldous Huxley was acutely conscious of the role of what he called the "ferocious ideologies" of the interwar period, especially fascism and communism. Modern ideologies like socialism, liberalism, or Marxism were, for the most part, secular systems of belief. As the products of an increasingly pluralist society, one in which the traditional framework of a universally held religion had collapsed in the face of challenges from science and technology, especially in the political and industrial revolutions of the late eighteenth and early nineteenth centuries, they claimed to know how best to organize and transform society. The emphasis of the Enlightenment on the presumably universal ideas of reason and science, the increase in literacy and communications, and the gradual extension of democratic rights created the historical context for the rise of such secular ideologies. Associated with specific groups or classes, each claimed, on the basis of self-justifying appeals to science and reason, that its vision of society and its historical goals were the correct ones.

Huxley, observing the intensifying rivalry of political parties and sectarian systems during the late twenties and early thirties, became increasingly critical of his contemporaries' addiction to what he called "insane ideals." The new romantic trend that he claimed to detect throughout modern society was a blanket term for materialism, Russian communism, and the twentieth century's love of technological innovation. Such presumably rationalist and objective values screened more irrational impulses and interests. "But men are not content to desire; they like to have a logical or pseudo-logical justification for their desires; they like to believe that when they want something, it is not merely for their own personal advantage, but that their desires are dictated by pure reason, by nature, by God Himself. The greater part of the world's philosophy and theology is merely an intellectual justification for the wishes and the day-dreams of philosophers and theologians. And practically all political theories are elaborated, after the fact, to justify the interests and desires of certain individuals, classes, or nations."[82] This is a remarkable passage that stresses precisely those factors informing the most recent discussions of ideology.[83] Huxley emphasizes that the philosophical beliefs of his contemporaries are ideological for two reasons: First, they claim to be complete, natural, and necessary; that is, they are offered as logical or logically entailed, hence "necessary." Second, they are presented as natural or rooted in nature (part of the way things are or the order of things). But, Huxley maintains, in reality, they are screens or surface justifications that mask a hidden or latent desire that, in turn, is linked to the interests of "certain individuals, classes, or nations." Appearing to assert a logical and coherent interpretation of human aspiration, they are, in reality, the artificial, illogical, and incomplete expression of the interests of special groups. Far from being natural, an ideology is a fabricated and contingent political philosophy, the goal of which is the attainment of power to satisfy a particular sectarian agenda. In novels like *Point Counter Point* and *Eyeless in Gaza*, Huxley focused on the "insane ideals" and "ferocious ideologies" of his contemporaries. In *Brave New World* he continued this critique but with a sharper focus on the ideology of science. His principal concern was the new romantic worship of science, technology, and mechanization, especially as it promoted these as a screen for socioeconomic power. *Brave New World* is a vision of a future dominated by instrumental reason, by carefully circumscribed technology, and by a class of administrative technocrats who claim to understand human desire. Such a select scientific elite is the ultimate expression of new romantic values. The utopia it creates is a grotesque projection into the future of what Huxley saw as his contemporaries' misplaced faith in technical and bureaucratic expertise that could only result in the "spiritual self-mutilation"[84] of the race.

In 1937, Stephen Spender, in *Forward from Liberalism*, accused the English middle class of exhibiting a "sentimental masochism" symptomatized by a cultural "death wish."[85] In *The Thirties: 1930– 1940*, written in the final years of the decade, Malcolm Muggeridge wrote of a "longing for death" and "a reservoir of death-longing, ready to be tapped" in the minds and hearts of his contemporaries.[86] Well after the thirties, Sir Herbert Read, looking back on this period, especially the years after the First World War, observed that "the death wish that was once an intellectual fiction" had "become a hideous reality."[87] Huxley, noted earlier, had asserted that "the new romanticism . . . [was] headed straight towards death." This cultural mood, based on the rather melodramatic metaphor of a social death wish, was linked in Huxley's mind with "the insane ideals" energizing the competing ideologies of the thirties. Suicides and self-destructive social types crowd the pages of his novels. In *Brave New World*, the Savage not only hangs himself but exhibits pronounced sadomasochistic traits, a conjunction of suicide and sadomasochism that lies at the heart of Huxley's diagnosis of what he called "the disease of modern man." In an essay entitled "Accidie," published in *On the Margin* (1923), he noted what he regarded as the markedly intense anomie of the modern period. Anomie or accidie refers not only to a collapse of social organization but, in particular, to the psychological symptoms of such a state, alienation and antisocial behavior. Huxley observed among his contemporaries a "sense of universal futility, the feeling of boredom and despair, with the complementary desire to be 'anywhere, anywhere out of the world' " and asked, "What is the significance of this fact? For clearly the progress of accidie is a spiritual event of considerable importance. How is it to be explained?"[88] Huxley explained it, as we have seen, by means of his concept of psychological trends and his theory of modern romanticism. But the concept of social anomie and the motif of suicide and sadomasochistic behavior was derived from his fascination with the Marquis de Sade.

In his letter to George Orwell comparing the dystopian prophecies of *Nineteen Eighty-Four* and *Brave New World,* Huxley observed that Orwell's vision of a future totalitarian state described, in fact, a stage in a process of historical events that would eventually "modulate into the nightmare of a world having more resemblance to that which I imagined in *Brave New World.*" The principal reason for this further development lay with what Huxley called "the ultimate revolution." He defined this final historical possibility as one of the "total subversion" of the individual's mind and body and linked it to the values of the Marquis de Sade. For Huxley, this eighteenth-century French aristocrat was the quintessential nihilist, a sensual materialist obsessed with the human body and a proponent of a bleak philosophy of systematic cynicism. De Sade's life was one of repeated acts of sexual transgression alternating with brief spells of imprisonment. His bizarre sexual preferences included rape, kidnapping, and torture, which he celebrated in his novels and enthusiastically practiced in his own life. His importance for Huxley lay in his belief that human morality was a fiction, that human beings were isolated, egocentric individuals motivated solely by personal desire. The only relationship that de Sade recognized was that of victim and victimizer; carnal concupiscence and violence were the basic premises of the materialist philosophy of sensual self-gratification which he celebrated in pornographic novels like *Justine.* Huxley employed de Sade and sadomasochism in his nov-

els of the interwar period as a symbol of cultural decline, of the collapse of moral belief and social conventions. Characters who exhibited
sadomasochistic traits or symptoms were, in a manner of speaking,
carriers of what Huxley called "the disease of modern man." The
materialism and self-destructive violence of the new romanticism were
dramatized by a series of sexually violent grotesques, beginning with
Coleman in *Antic Hay* and reaching their most virulently Sadean form
with the Earl of Gonister in *After Many a Summer Dies the Swan*.

The Marquis de Sade was linked to Huxley's criticism of the
concept of historical progress in that de Sade had become Huxley's
symbol of twentieth-century materialism, especially as it manifested
itself in what he had come to regard as the self-destructive ideologies
of the interwar period. De Sade's nihilism was the final degenerative
stage of the systematic rationalization of the desire for power and
mastery that Huxley detected in contemporary political mass movements. In this respect, the Sadean lust for power was one of the lasting
consequences of a process of cultural decline inaugurated during the
romantic period and, especially, by the French revolution of 1789.
Huxley's explanation of the progress of accidie or anomie in contemporary European society was simply the course of European "history
since 1789," a process of degeneration given additional momentum by
"the appalling catastrophe of the War of 1914."[89] In Huxley's mind,
de Sade came to assume the stature of a sociological type whose "madness illuminates the dark places of normal behavior" as well as the
social and cultural climate of the thirties. In *Ends and Means* Huxley
described de Sade as the proponent of a "philosophy of meaninglessness" based on a denial "of any values, any idealism, any binding
moral imperatives whatsoever."[90] In short, he exemplified what Huxley called the "nihilist revolution,"[91] a spiritual aimlessness rooted in
an ideology of meaninglessness that, on the level of the individual,
engendered irrational and self-destructive behavior and, on the level of
society, manifested itself as cultural accidie.

In *Ends and Means* Huxley described the thirties as oscillating
between Sadean cynicism and accidie on the one hand and the "ferocious ideologies" of communism and fascism on the other. "The

'heads' of pointlessness has as its 'tails' idolatrous nationalism and communism. Our world oscillates from a neurasthenia that welcomes war as a relief from boredom to a mania that results in war being made."[92] As the proponent of a systematically conceived cynicism, of "ultimate revolution," de Sade was a philosopher who denied human claims to importance and morality and a psychotic whose violent impulses and voyeuristic stances were adopted by a number of Huxley's characters, including the Savage of *Brave New World*. De Sade's elaboration of a "philosophy of meaninglessness carried to its logical conclusion" corresponded, in Huxley's mind, to the general anomic condition of European society in the aftermath of the Great War, when "the philosophy of meaninglessness came once more triumphantly into fashion."[93] Sadomasochistic behavior, then, is a central motif in Huxley's satire and dominates the latter half of *Brave New World*. It is a symbol of social decadence as well as a psychological perversion associated with erotic violence, anomic suicide, and the "lust for power" that Huxley saw as the animating bias of European politics. It can also be linked to Huxley's attack on the materialism informing the collectivist ideologies of Marxism and the excesses of American capitalism in that Huxley regarded de Sade's extreme cynicism as rooted in a debasing materialism where "sensations and animal pleasures alone possessed reality and were alone worth living for."[94] Such a stress on sensual hedonism is the foundation of the society depicted in *Brave New World*.

Huxley's antipathy for Marxist and fascist ideology is tied, at least in part, to his distaste for the mass politics of the thirties. His dislike of what he saw as the mass movements surrounding dictators like Mussolini, Stalin, and Hitler, however, did not proceed from a traditionally liberal belief in individualism, democracy, or progressivist theories of history. In an essay entitled "Progress," published in 1928 in *Vanity Fair*, Huxley described the liberal notion of historical progress as a secular ideology made possible by, first, the collapse of the worldview of medieval and renaissance Christianity and, second, by the "enormous expansion of man's material resources during the age of industrialism." Such a belief in the progressive improvement of

61

the cultural as well as the material basis of civilization was, he argued, an illusion. Such an illusion was based on an identification of technological advancement with intellectual and ethical development. But history, he maintained, was not "orthogenetic," that is, it showed no bias in "one particular direction." Insofar as "history and the at all predictable future" were concerned, he insisted that there was "no such thing as a specific and heritable progress."[95] What there was was incessant change but "without ameliorative direction."[96] Huxley's repudiation of uncritical notions of progress was in line with the views of many of his contemporaries, for whom liberalism and its meliorist theories of history had been discredited by events in Russia, Germany, and throughout Europe. But Huxley's criticism was directed at one of the linchpins of the belief in the gradualist advancement of civilization, the primacy of science and technology.

8

Science and Utopia:
Bertrand Russell, Max Weber, and
Huxley's Technocratic Dystopia

One of the possible sources of Huxley's ideas concerning science, its methodology, and its cultural or ideological goals is Bertrand Russell's *The Scientific Outlook,* published in 1931. It has been argued, most notably by Philip Thody, that *Brave New World* derives almost all of its originality from this source, to the extent that it is questionable "if Huxley put any original ideas into his book."[97] Peter Firchow has suggested the opposite, that Russell may, in fact, have borrowed his ideas from Huxley.[98] The question of influence between Russell and Huxley resembles the charges of indebtedness, even plagiarism, leveled against both Orwell and Huxley in relation to Zamiatin's *We.* It can best be resolved, again, by emphasizing the role of genre and the development of the twentieth-century utopia. Many of Russell's ideas bear some resemblance to those of H. G. Wells; indeed, they involve issues that would inevitably be raised in any modern work purporting to be a utopian or dystopian vision of the future. Thody is, nevertheless, correct in noting the sheer number of critical points of contact between Russell's description of a scientifically organized "world State" and Huxley's depiction of a highly centralized, technocratic "World State."

Russell's *The Scientific Outlook* was both a serious attempt to explore the political and ethical implications for society of recent advances in science and technology, and a tongue-in-cheek satire of scientific ambition. Russell warned that his nonfiction study was not to be taken "altogether as serious prophecy"; he defined it as "an attempt to depict the world which would result if scientific technique were to rule unchecked."[99] Such an aim obviously accords with Huxley's *Brave New World* or Zamiatin's *We*. But Russell's intent (like Huxley's) was not merely to inventory the technological marvels of modern science, nor was he concerned with contemporary issues of scientific methodology, although he does discuss these in some detail. What fascinated Russell was the issue of power as it related to the emergence of Soviet Russia and the United States as modern technocracies, that is, as states whose wealth and power depended on the practical employment of scientific technique. The pivotal concept of Russell's dystopia, his "prophecy" of a scientific "world State," was the concept of power, which he conceived as the ability to manipulate nature on an unprecedentedly massive scale. The result of recent advances in scientific technique was, he feared, its elevation into a political and social philosophy of instrumentality. What troubled Russell was the prospect of a wholesale extension of scientific technique, normally directed at the natural world, into the realm of social and political organization. What underlay such a development was the desire for mastery and control that seemed inseparable from science.

Russell complained that "our age is one which increasingly substitutes power for the older ideals, and this is happening in science as elsewhere."[100] H. G. Wells, in his utopian novels, consistently focused on science as a state of mind, a vital energy manifesting itself as "an insatiable appetite for knowledge and habitual creative urgency," as noted earlier. The key words here are "appetite" and "urgency." Wells viewed nature as a phenomenon to be controlled and eventually mastered. Nature was inherently fluid, disorganized, without will or purpose. With humanity came the impulse to control and manipulate, to analyze, dominate, and, finally, to master. In his utopian novels, like *Men Like Gods*, Wells never exhibited much awareness of the aggressive emphasis on domination and control that resides within the scientific mentality—especially in the area of applied science and technology. Russell and Huxley, however, were in agreement on this issue. For Russell, science was "the pursuit of power," while for Huxley, the "lust for power" was the principal motivating force in modern European history. But power was not simply a matter of means or neutral technique. Rather, Russell argued, "Modern technique has given man a sense of power which is rapidly altering his whole mentality." He maintained that to the typical modern mind what a thing is is of no interest in and of itself. On the contrary, it inspires interest only on account of "what it may be made to become." For Russell, modern science had been created by men of the seventeenth century who valued scientific discovery for its own sake, and who were motivated by a disinterested love of knowledge. Twentieth-century science, however, had become tainted by what he claimed was a scientific will to power. "In psychological terms, this means that the love of power has thrust aside all the other impulses that make the complete human life."[101] Such a deformation of human nature, he argued, is ultimately transferred to society itself. Accordingly, the appearance of new social organizations such as Russell's world State are premised on the political connection between the scientist and industrialist. "All modern scientific thinking," he claimed, "is at bottom power thinking." The desire to control nature, reinforced by the recent advances in scientific technique, leads inevitably to the desire to control and regulate society. In this regard the interests of the scientist and the ruling industrialist converge in Russell's conception of the centralized world State where "manipulation and exploitation are the ruling passions of the typical scientific industrialist."[102]

Russell's dystopia or world State, like Zamiatin's One State, Huxley's World State, and Orwell's Oceania, is dedicated to the preservation of social stability. It is, in essence, an oligarchy, a government by a small faction wholly dedicated to the preservation of the stable status quo. Russell believed that most scientists were "citizens first, and servants of truth only in the second place." This, as we shall see, is a fairly accurate description of Mustapha Mond, one of the leading oligarchs of Huxley's World State. The society that Russell envisioned was an inevitable result of increasing technical specialization, whereby the dependency of the population on various technologies such as scientific agriculture, medicine, and food distribution gradually required increasingly sophisticated patterns of organization. "The social effect of modern scientific technique is, in practically all directions, to demand an increase both in the size and intensity of organization."[103] The resulting dystopian culture that Russell envisaged was the consequence of the rise of scientific specialists, technocrats who would eventually take control of existing political structures. The ascendancy of the scientific expert was the inevitable result of what Russell saw as a radical increase in the size and complexity of modern industrial society. The urgent need for the effective application of scientific expertise to essentially technical problems within the context of mass industrial society would, he believed, create a radically new culture.

Russell's depiction of a scientific world State introduces the last and perhaps the most revealing feature of the early twentieth-century dystopia, a characteristic present in Wells's utopias but not deeply probed until the appearance of novels like *We, Brave New World,* and *Nineteen Eighty-Four.* The discussion in chapter 4 stressed the various oppositions, such as reason and feeling, that inform the Wellsian utopian novel and its later variants. Russell's *Scientific Outlook,* however, focuses on a final but all-important aspect of the modern dystopia, the rise of modern bureaucracy and the appearance of the totalitarian bureaucratic state (especially the Soviet Union with its immense party apparatus). Wells touched on this problem in his dystopias such as *The Sleeper Awakes,* but only briefly. He simply assumed that a scientific culture of experts would act in harmony without the need of governmental organizations. As the Utopians of *Men Like Gods* naively proclaimed: "*Our education is our government.*" Russell, Zamiatin, and Huxley were not so convinced of the political innocence of scientists or their neutral role in the use of the state's technology. It is this fear of benign, bureaucratic coercion that, as we shall see, makes *Brave New World* a political novel as well as a dark fantasy of the future.

Russell's world State is the result of the inexorable expansion of technological and bureaucratic power. The paradigmatic expression of such a historical development was, for Russell, the Soviet Union; its spokesman was Lenin, and its principal innovation was its new ethic of secular technocracy. As early as 1920 Russell had described the Soviet government as a powerful bureaucracy notable chiefly for its "truly terrible degree of centralization" and its devotion to self-perpetuating power.[104] By 1931, the year in which *The Scientific Outlook* first appeared, Stalin had taken complete control of both the Party and state apparatus; he had inaugurated the first Five Year Plan in 1928 and issued the collectivization decree in 1929. The Soviet Union, under the authoritarian rule of one man, had launched itself on a program to reorganize and expand Russian industry, to mechanize its agriculture, and to create a socialist technocracy. Russell saw the U.S.S.R. as a precursor to his own scientific world state, all of its features requiring only further intensification and development. These features are worth noting, not because they may have influenced Huxley, who also regarded the Soviet Union as the product of what he called the new romanticism, with its emphasis on mechanization and technology, but because they are the fundamental ideological features of the early twentieth-century dystopia. In this respect, they highlight the role of socialist Russia in the novels of Zamiatin, Huxley, and Orwell. Equally important, when viewed collectively, they show that Russell was not an influence on Huxley in any simple or direct way, because Russell's Soviet-inspired world State resembles Zamiatin's of 1924 as much as Huxley's of 1932. Their mutual resemblance, then, is generic, and can be traced to the presiding historical anxieties of the interwar period—as Huxley always insisted.

Whatever their differences, early twentieth-century authors of dystopian narratives shared a deep skepticism on the subject of socialism, progress, and technology. Their wariness about the alliance of government and science, the politican and the technical expert, was shared by the German sociologist Max Weber. His *Protestant Ethic and the Spirit of Capitalism,* published in 1920, was widely read by British writers in the interwar period, and his ideas concerning modern bureaucracy in *Economy and Society* are of considerable relevance to the dystopian novel. Weber's interest in bureaucracy stemmed from his belief that the expansion of bureaucratic authority in the early twentieth century was a major threat to liberal values, particularly individual, creative freedom. In his attempt to identify the major features of bureaucracy, he isolated four defining traits: first, hierarchy (clear definition of work competency and responsibility to superiors); second, continuity (permanent employment with advancement opportunities); third, impersonality (work carried out according to codified rules and without favoritism); fourth and most important, expertise (officials are specialists and the product of a meritocratic system of education and advancement).[105] Weber was a social scientist who stressed the dangers of overorganization, especially as it tended toward systematic coercion or what he called "the iron cage" of bureaucracy. His key concept was the principle of rationalization. Society, he maintained, moved inevitably in the direction of more complex forms of organization, subjecting itself to more complicated codes and rules conducive to social control and the suppression of spontaneity and creativity. Russell was clearly indebted to Weber; *The Scientific Outlook* contains many of his ideas. Aldous Huxley probably absorbed Weberian ideas through Russell and Vilfredo Pareto's *The Mind and Society* (1916).

In an essay published eleven years after *Brave New World*, Huxley cogently summarized this historical convergence of bureaucracy and authoritarian power when he observed that modern historical tendencies were exhibiting "a steady increase in the power of the Big Shepherd and his oligarchy of bureaucratic dogs." Such a trend, he maintained, was inevitably contributing "to a growth in the size, the complexity, the machine-like efficiency and rigidity of social organizations, and to a completer deification of the State, accompanied by a completer reification, or reduction to thing-hood, of individual persons."[106] The inhabitants of Huxley's World State in *Brave New World* are meticulously subordinated to the institutionalized coercions analyzed by Weber. His dystopian state is fundamentally bureaucratic in its vertical, hierarchical structure based on intellectual competency (Alphas, Betas, Deltas, etc.). It exemplifies Weber's continuity in offering all of its citizens permanent security within an elaborate corporate structure. It is equally Weberian in its impersonality, its denial of personal identity and its insistence on social conformity. Most important, it is a technocracy of experts who have channeled their efforts toward the creation of a world of stable routine and economic efficiency.

Weber regarded such modern systems of large-scale administration, with their emphasis on expert or specialist knowledge, as, in David Beetham's phrase, "the archtypically modern institution." Such a structure can be found in governmental organizations or departments (e.g., the Pentagon, the CIA) or business corporations (e.g., The Ford Motor Company, IBM). However, according to Weber, bureaucracy is symptomatic of a tendency within modern society as a whole. The danger lies in its monopoly of expertise, its tendency to expand, and its emphasis on technology and instrumental values. Russell and Huxley saw in this potentially menacing convergence of scientific expertise and governmental bureaucracy the ideological basis for their totalitarian utopias and scientific world states. And while Weber feared the power of bureaucracies to undermine or wholly supplant representative forms of government, Huxley, in some of his essays written at the end of the 1920s, regarded this as inevitable, and in *Brave New World* he vividly dramatized what Weber especially feared, the static nature of the bureaucratic state, inherently conservative, inalterably opposed to change, innovation, and the risk-taking spirit of the genuinely creative scientist, politician, or industrialist. "The central question," Weber wrote, "is what we can oppose to this machinery, in order to keep a portion of humanity free from this pigeon-holing of the spirit, from this total domination of the bureaucratic ideal."[107]

In *The Scientific Outlook* Russell described the Soviet Union as an oligarchy of technical specialists, scientists, and administration or Party functionaries. As a highly centralized authoritarian society, the U.S.S.R., with its state system of education, its weakening of the family in favor of loyalty to the state, and its opposition to religion and traditional beliefs, was an important stage on the historical path to Russell's "organized world State." The key to the establishment of such a presumably utopian entity lay with the willingness of scientists to ally themselves with powerful industrial and governmental interests. Russell believed this was happening in the Soviet state, where all major elements of production and distribution were controlled by a centralized bureaucracy dedicated to technological progress, materialist values, and, above all, social stability. As Russell emphasized, and Huxley dramatized in *Brave New World*, the Soviet government carefully supervised technical research and disparaged the concept of pure science.

In Russell's model, the bureaucratic technocracy was founded on a state monopoly of expertise and a general philosophy of instrumentalism, that is, the privileging of technological means over ethically conceived ends. The ruling elite of his scientific world State was situated at the top of a monolithic hierarchy of a politically conservative character. Within such a Weberian "iron cage," the average citizen, unable to master one, much less all, of the areas of scientific expertise necessary to the survival of a modern state, would feel increasingly helpless. The political result would be the gradual relinquishing of the citizen's role in determining public policy. In a society where there was no equality of knowledge there could be no equality of political participation. Russell predicted that eventually an oligarchy would acquire global domination, producing "a world-wide organization as complete and elaborate as that now existing in the U.S.S.R."[108] The impulse behind such a development was not simply the necessity for coping with the complex demands of industrial mass society. Russell argued that science, as it turned from the realm of pure research and entered into the sphere of applying that knowledge under the direction of a ruling elite, became contaminated with ideology. His insistence, noted earlier, that "all modern scientific thinking is at bottom power thinking" and his belief that "most scientists were citizens first, and servants of truth only in the second place" were integral to his vision of a dystopian world state. Science, in its urge to master nature, could easily be deflected to a desire to master humanity. Russell feared the "social effect of modern scientific technique," arguing that such manipulative skills were "likely to lead to a governmental tyranny." And

Science and Utopia

such a "scientific society," he claimed, would "be just as oligarchic under socialism or communism as under capitalism."[109]

Such a dark utopia would require a special kind of scientific ideologue, a man like Lenin whom Russell saw as an "idealistic manipulator." Lenin was, he argued, the quintessential technocrat whose political thinking was governed by a "new ethic which is gradually growing in connection with scientific technique." Such pragmatic idealists would reject the illusory values of liberalism in favor of the "complicated mechanism of a modern community," where the scientific bureaucracy would govern every aspect of communal existence. The primary goal of such a state would be stability. To achieve it, the state would require an ideology, or what Russell called "an official metaphysic," stressing materialism, comfort, and security within a closed world of social regimentation and hierarchical authority. The "new ethic" for the growing bureaucracy would be the celebration of "the art of scientific manipulation."[110]

Russell believed that social engineering, central planning, and the impulse to regulate and control complex political and social organizations were rooted in a more asocial and sinister desire: "The power impulse is embodied in industrialism and its governmental technique. It is embodied also in the philosophies known as pragmatism and instrumentalism." Equally important, he believed that "in the development of science the power impulse has increasingly prevailed."[111] The fundamental drive to exploit and control the physical world of nature converges, in Russell's view, with the impulse to control humanity within socially stable organizations. He believed that the example of such a merging of natural science and political or social instrumentalism could be found in the behaviorist psychology of J. B. Watson and Ivan Pavlov. The future state that Russell envisioned was only possible on the basis of major development in psychological conditioning and experimental embryology. J. B. Watson's *Behaviorism* (1925) and *The Battle of Behaviorism* (1928) elaborated a mechanistic psychology based on the premise that mental activity was confined to psychological responses to stimuli. Russell noted that such a psychology, stressing "an apparatus of reflexes and the process of condition-

71

ing," was, in fact, "a technique for acquiring power" that embodied "the methods which have always been adopted by those who train animals or drill soldiers."[112] Such a psychology, when combined with advances in embryology, would permit not only extensive social conditioning but prenatal education, a possibility dramatized by Huxley in *Brave New World*, where one of his characters is named after Watson and genetic engineering has become a necessary part of the social order.

Russell's scientific world State, then, is Wellsian to the extent that it is described as a society where the "experts" compose the "real government." Such a "close corporation" of technocrats would have created a carefully stratified society, pyramidal in structure, with the vast base composed of a passive working class population.[113] As in Wells's *The Sleeper Awakes* and Huxley's *Brave New World*, social grades would be determined according to the kind of work to be performed. Scientifically conditioned to accept their status as industrial workers, members of the working class would be intellectually brutalized and encouraged to devote their spare time to "endless amusements." The study of history would be unnecessary because the citizens of Russell's world State would be trained to feel for the past only contempt, as in Huxley's *Brave New World*, where history is a forbidden subject. The ruling oligarchy would proscribe humanistic study, including "such works as *Hamlet* and *Othello*," while new forms of drugs and intoxicants, like Huxley's *soma*, would be systematically distributed for the purpose of social control.[114]

In such a world of cooperative, standardized social behavior, intellectual or scientific initiative would be impossible even among the bureaucratic elite. Only technical research devoted to the preservation of the order and stability of the state would be permitted, and even that would be carefully monitored. The result of such uniformity of opinion, reinforced by mass media, cinema, and various forms of propaganda, would be a degree of social stability indistinguishable from that of a beehive. The presiding ideology of such a state, where the bureaucratic goals of security, control, resistance to change, and hierarchical structure based on technical expertise have assumed the status of an official state religion, is exemplified in what Russell called "the industrial mentality" and personified, he argued, in men like Edison, Rockefeller, and Lenin. This conjunction of two American capitalists and a Russian Marxist as representative of the mentality informing the ruling elite of Russell's global oligarchy is characteristic of the ideology informing the modern dystopia.

The connection between the United States and the Soviet Union exemplified in Russell's linking of Rockefeller and Lenin is a leitmotiv in the essays of Huxley, whose criticism of American and Soviet civilization closely resembles Russell's. Huxley's assessment of American society, particularly as it illuminates aspects of *Brave New World,* can be found at its most succinct in "The Outlook for American Culture," published in *Harpers Magazine* in August of 1927, and in "Whither Are We Civilizing?" in the April 1928 issue of *Vanity Fair.* These two essays, with those reprinted in *Proper Studies* and *Music at Night,* offer a reasonably representative view of what Huxley regarded as the "Americanized world"[115] of the interwar decades. Like Russell, he saw the world confronting a choice between Russian and American values. In his speculations on the role of the United States in modern history, however, he maintained that America was not unique; it merely led the world in science, technology, and industry. Europe, he argued, held the same or very similiar values. As a result, America was Europe's, if not the world's, future; in short, it revealed the cloudy lineaments of a distant utopia, however partial and blurred. In "The Outlook for American Culture" he observed that "the future of America is the future of the world," but added that "prophecies of the future, if they are to be intelligent, not merely fantastic, must be based on a study of the present. The future is the present projected."[116] *Brave New World* is such a projection of the American present, conflating Huxley's critique of American "material democracy" with his concerns about the Soviet bureaucratic state.

Huxley regarded the United States as a somewhat benign plutocracy in which technological innovation and mass production techniques had made it possible for "capitalists who control it to impose whatever ideas and art-forms they please on the mass of humanity."

Such an unbending pursuit of wealth through the technique of mass production found its most adequate symbol in the assembly lines of the Ford Motor Company. More important, the men who controlled such techniques were, he believed, part of the governing class. Just as the Russian state had degenerated after the revolution into a monolithic bureaucracy governed by a party elite, so, in the United States, Huxley maintained, power had tended "to be concentrated in the hands of intelligent and active oligarchies." Huxley regarded such a trend as inevitable and believed that the American system retained one great advantage. If it was oligarchic in terms of the distribution of power, it was also a meritocracy that permitted the rise of talented individuals. "The great merit of the American system," he wrote, "consists solely in this—that careers are open to the talents." Nevertheless, he believed that the genuinely ideal government had to be both meritocratic and democratic, a difficult synthesis. "The ideal state is one in which there is a material democracy controlled by an aristocracy of intellect—a state in which men and women are guaranteed a decent human existence and are given every opportunity to develop such talents as they possess, and where those with the greatest talent rule."[117] The problem, of course, was whether the talented few could be trusted to govern the less talented many. Equally important, how was talent to be defined? And would the emphasis on technical instrumentation, considering what Russell stressed as its motivating desire for mastery and power, permit the free exercise of intellect?

In *Proper Studies* Huxley observed that "the intellectually gifted are notorious for the ruthless way in which they cultivate their gifts, regardless of what the rest of the world may think or desire."[118] In *Brave New World* Huxley painted a much darker picture of the ideal state described in "The Outlook for American Culture." Always assuming that the historical "basis for all civilization is technology," Huxley envisioned in his essays a more optimistically conceived community, reasonably liberal and democratic to the extent of guaranteeing equal opportunity as well as universal legal protection. In such a society all would have the education they were "fitted to receive" and all would enjoy the "humanitarian" benefits of a technologically advanced society. But what he regarded as the deeply flawed political democracy of England and the United States of the late twenties would be replaced by "more efficient and rational forms of government." America he praised as the most democratic as well as "the most highly technized of any country,"[119] yet, like the Soviet Union, it fell well short of his utopian meritocracy.

Finally, a second passage must be laid beside the definition of the "ideal state" quoted earlier, because of its relevance to *Brave New World*. The need for efficiency and rationality in government was to be met by the technical specialist, the expert who was endowed with administrative power to set and coordinate policy. As one of those "fitted to receive" the scientific and technical education necessary to the achievement of the state's goals, the expert's status was ambiguous and divided: "In modern civilized societies the man, in Rousseau's words, is sacrificed to the citizen—the whole instinctive, emotional, psychological being is sacrificed to the specialized, intellectual part of every man."[120] This passage appeared in Huxley's essay "Whither Are We Civilizing?" published in the April 1928 issue of *Vogue*. It can be regarded as the thematic point of departure for *Brave New World* to the extent that it poses the fundamental question raised in a somewhat different form by Russell and Weber. Modern technocratic societies run the risk of encouraging the psychological deformity of the over-specialized expert and his or her love of mastery, order, and power. The "spiritual self-mutilation" inflicted by modern industrial societies on their citizens as a consequence of mechanistic technology, especially when employed by men like Henry Ford, is a pervasive theme in *Brave New World*. The distinction between intellect and feeling in the modern dystopias of Huxley, Zamiatin, and Russell is linked to the rise of the technical specialist and the fear that if scientific experts have sacrificed feeling or instinct on the altar of reason, they might not hesitate to sacrifice the lives of those whom they govern as well. As Huxley noted in *Proper Studies*, "How far it is possible for any one in a modern, highly organized society of specialists to be, in Rousseau's phrase, both a man and a citizen is doubtful."[121]

Huxley rejected the older liberal values such as the belief that, at least in theory, men and women are reasonable and naturally equal, that they are, if not indefinitely educable, at least capable of achieving a significant state of intellectual enlightenment, and that they are products of their environment.[122] The meritocratic alternative, however, was no guarantee of a humanely rational community. Huxley's confidence in what he called "the aristocratic ideal—the ideal that the naturally best men should be at the top" could not be separated from his belief in the "ruthless way" in which "the intellectually gifted" pursue their ostensibly creative ends.[123] In *Brave New World* the men at the top are not as crudely appetitive as Zamiatin's or Orwell's power-hungry ideologues; their pursuit of control and stability manifests itself in more subtle modes of behavior. But the state that they supervise is a hierarchical one, rigidly meritocratic and founded on the specialized knowledge of the scientist. It is also—paradoxically—a collectivist community where "every one belongs to every one else." In short, it is the product of Lenin and Ford, of new romantic bolshevism and American industrial standardization.

In *Discipline and Punish,* Michel Foucault challenged the traditional notion of utopia by suggesting that there have always been two competing ideals of a perfect society. "Historians of ideas usually attribute the dream of a perfect society to the philosophers and jurists of the eighteenth century; but there was also a military dream of society; its fundamental reference was not to the state of nature, but to the meticulously subordinated cogs of a machine, not to the primal social contract, but to permanent coercions, not to fundamental rights, but to indefinitely progressive forms of training, not to the general will but to automatic docility."[124] Huxley's World State is not a military dream of disciplined regimentation, but it is a world of machines, of coglike automatons who exist within a sphere of ubiquitous coercion. They live in a society shaped by science so completely and absolutely that they are, in a literal sense, its very products. Such an ideal of perfection turns on a notion of power and stability undreamt of by H. G. Wells, yet present, embryolike, in his untroubled visions of a scientific paradise.

Part 2
Brave New World

9

Huxley and Henry Ford: Chapters 1–2

Brave New World opens with a vision of unnaturally induced birth and closes with an artificially contrived death. This basic opposition shapes the structure of Huxley's novel, where the presumed advances of technological and scientific research have finally given birth to a universal state that, on its appearance, signals the death of history and creative freedom. The introductory scene in the Central London Hatchery and Conditioning Centre focuses on the intertwined themes of science and progress, as the Director of Hatcheries lectures a group of students on the workings of the Centre and its various departments. Chapters 1 and 2 are dominated by his technical analysis of the workings of the Hatchery. Chapter 3 introduces the key figure of Mustapha Mond, who instructs the students on the history of the World State. This chapter culminates in a montage of voices that collectively expresses the social texture and cultural values of this supposedly utopian society. After these opening chapters, the narrative pace quickens in its dramatization of the life of Bernard Marx, the first of the novel's two central protagonists. Chapters 1 and 2 provide the thematic key to much of what follows.

The Director's running commentary on the technological achievements of the World State takes place in the controlled and ordered space of the laboratory. With its gleaming white porcelain, its ranked equipment and polished surfaces, it stands at the beginning of Huxley's narrative as a triumphant symbol of the World State's trust in the power of rational instrumentality. Nature has been displaced by the artificial products of reason, and the most complex of natural processes, the reproductive cycle of conception and birth, has been mastered by genetic engineering and artificial insemination. The tour of the Hatchery itself replicates the birth process; it begins in the Fertilizing Room and proceeds through the Bottling Room, the Social Predestination Room, the Embryo Store, and the Decanting Room, and finally ends at the Nurseries. The movement of the students is accompanied by rows of bottles on a moving conveyor belt, a feature of the Hatchery that emphasizes the degree to which the scientific laboratory has merged with the industrial production line. The interior of the Hatchery is a world of controlled temperatures, muffled sounds, and carefully adjusted lighting that suggests the enclosed serenity of the womb. Far more important, however, is the simple fact that natural processes have been displaced by technology to the extent that the citizens of the World State are literally conceived by science, not by individual men and women. They are born within an impersonal system of subjection that determines their future, their intellectual and psychological traits, and, as a result, their social status while still in an embryonic form. This human nightmare is the scientific bureaucrat's dream of social order, of the mastery of nature that merges imperceptibly with the political mastery of humanity as well.

The Director, then, is a Wellsian spokesman for the new order, surrounded by his apprentice sorcerers who are busy mixing, maturing, and decanting a witch's brew of artificially evolved human types. His lecture is a technical explanation and a historical narrative combined in a sermon celebrating the ideology of the World State. The ideological context of his lecture can be located in what amounts to an elaboration of the World State's motto: "Community, Identity, Stability" (1). Russell, in *The Scientific Outlook*, had argued that the scientific bureaucrat would value stability as the fundamental goal of society. The motto places the key term, "Identity," within the bracketing embrace of the collectivist ideals of the World State, "Community" and "Stability." In such a culture, individual identity is only permissible within a social and collectivist setting (community); moreover, within a community that is fixed and unchanging (stability). Such a technocratic ideal is, as Huxley argued, a form of "spiritual self-mutilation," and thus the laboratory, dedicated to birth, is depicted as a place of death and genetic deformation. The light is "frozen, dead, a ghost," while the lab technicians wear "corpse-coloured rubber." Outside it is summer but within all is "wintriness" (1). The laboratory is a scientific womb, displacing the mythical maternal nature with the colder fertilizing embrace of scientific instrumentalism.

It is not, however, a research laboratory, because pure experimental inquiry is sharply curtailed and monitored in the conservative World State. Surrounded by the mass-produced creatures of the Hatchery, the Director is a kind of Victor Frankenstein supervising the production of a wholly transformed and monstrous race. His first observation is to reject theoretical science and to proclaim the primacy of "particulars" or discrete facts: "For particulars, as everyone knows, make for virtue and happiness; generalities are intellectually necessary evils" (2). The superiority of applied science as opposed to pure research and theory is central to the ideology of the technocrat; it is the axiomatic basis of his power. But the Director is forced to contradict himself in that his attack on generalities is itself a generalization. As Huxley's narrative proceeds, a number of the citizens of this dogmatic technocracy will, for varying reasons, exhibit signs of contradictory behavior. This will be traceable either to the theoretical inconsistencies of World State ideology or to the emotional and intellectual frustrations of characters like Bernard Marx and Helmholtz Watson.

If the Director begins his lecture with a generalization against generalizations, he quickly proceeds to a discussion of history, with its broad generalizations about human origins, although History, as he knows, is a forbidden topic. His lecture is a historical summary of technological advances, and his phrase "begin at the beginning" is another political error in that it invokes prohibited subject matter (i.e., discussion of origins, biography, history, the past, childhood, etc.). His brief summation of Bokanovsky's Process—a method of increasing the rate of ovulation—is especially ironic in that it equates cultural "progress" with the technical means to induce "arrests of development" (5). The ability to manipulate the reproductive cycle to the extent of altering the genetic nature of embryos is, for the Director, not only the crowning achievement of the state, but its final one. It is not only the eggs that have been subjected to the arrested development. In the Director's world, history itself has come to a final and monstrously arrested climax.

The Director is a spokesman, then, for the hegemony of technology and instrumental reason, including the enforced conformities of World State science. Technological advances have significant political ramifications because, he claims, they are the "major instruments of social stability" (6). Equally important, technology aligns itself with commercial and industrial interests, the bokanovskification process, for example, being defined by the Director as "the principle of mass production at last applied to biology" (7). Social stability is achieved as the result of the ability to create, by means of genetic engineering, standardized classes of human beings denominated as Alphas, Betas, Gammas, Deltas, and Epsilons (as well as subcategories indicated by plus or minus signs). The result is a rigidly stratified society, hierarchical, rule governed, and conformist, in which authority is derived from expertise; in short, a vast social pyramid ruled by scientific specialists who worship Weber's bureaucrat's ideal of order, regimentation, and stability.

A second important feature of the Director's lecture—one that is fundamental to the dystopian novel—is the opposition between the artificial world of technology and the artless world of nature. The Director exults in the World State's rational instrumentality, which has brought society "out of the realm of mere slavish imitation of nature into the much more interesting world of human invention" (14). Nature, he argues, has been mastered, not simply by technology, but "on grounds of high economic policy" (24). The Director's disdain for "wild nature in general" is ideological as well as technological

Huxley and Henry Ford

because, as he complains, "a love of nature keeps no factories busy" (24)—an economic focus that introduces the role of Henry Ford in Huxley's dystopia. The first reference to Ford occurs in a discussion of the underlying economics of the World State, where the emphasis is on controlled markets, carefully accelerated rates of production, and the enforced consumption of commodities. The Director loves numbers; indeed, quantification is his principal mode of perception in a world where the production of socialized consumers is delicately scaled to the parallel production of commodities, and where the birth rate at the Hatcheries is regulated to match market consumption and production. The deification of Henry Ford within a kind of secular religion underscores the centrality of Taylorism (see below) in Huxley's vision of a technocracy where biology is an instrument of economic policy. Ford, then, as the World State's personification of triumphant technology, requires some brief discussion.

Between 1910 and 1920 Henry Ford's name had become synonymous with technical advances in industrial production. The appearance of the Model T in 1908 and the seemingly insatiable demand for Ford's product led to a series of innovations in production methods inspired by technical specialists like Walter Flanders and William Klann. By 1910 Ford's Highland Park plant in Detroit was the site of a revolution in assembly methods. The chief figure in the development of the techniques of mass production was Frederick W. Taylor, the "father of scientific management." He had revolutionized the American steel industry and, in 1911, published *The Principles of Scientific Management*. Taylor's theory of line production introduced the concept of rationalization into the workplace. It divided and subdivided factory labor into a system of simple functions or tasks, all carefully timed to ensure maximum efficiency and profit regardless of the effects on the worker. The brutalizing consequences of continually speeded up assembly lines, the firings of older workers who could not adjust to the new demands, and the sheer monotony and exhaustion of the simplified work were coldly viewed as irrelevant to the goals of mass production. Taylor's techniques were adopted and further refined by Henry Ford, who created not only a famous car but a method of production as sadistically brutal as it was financially successful. By 1914 Ford had introduced the continuous automatic conveyor, a moving belt that carried the entire production line and resulted in a completely assembled automobile in ninety-three minutes. By February of 1920, the Highland Park line was producing a car every minute; by 1925 a completed car rolled off the line every ten seconds.

Such a process of mass production was achieved at the expense of the worker. The Ford mechanic, who was once a skilled craftsman, was reduced to a mere assembler, a machine tender who labored monotonously at a rudimentary task for hours without a break. Workers quit the Ford plant in droves until Ford was forced to introduce the five-dollar day. With each new technical innovation, Ford increased the speed of the production line, firing workers who could not endure the speed of the production line only to rehire them at lower wages. He became known as "Henry Ford, the Speed-up King," the proprietor of a sweatshop, loathed by many of his employees and obsessed with profits.

Claiming that a "great business is really too big to be human," he established what came to be known as the "Ford Sociology Department," an office whose function was to monitor and spy on the personal lives of Ford employees in order to root out and expose moral failure. If the company investigators judged a worker to be wasting his money or living in a dissolute manner, his pay was cut or he was suspended. Such a system of supervision and surveillance, both on and off the job, when coupled with the brutalizing speed of production line work, had serious consequences. By the late 1920s the workers on the assembly lines had developed what came to be known as "the Ford stomach," a nervous condition generated by stress and exhaustion. Supervision in the factories had reached the point where talking with co-workers was forbidden, even during the lunch break. Prohibited from speaking, Ford workers devised what was called the "Ford whisper," a form of covert speech used on the assembly lines. Humming, whistling, even smiling while at work were regarded by the Ford Service of company spies as insubordination. In November of 1940, John Gallo, an employee at the Rouge Plant, was fired for smiling on the assembly line, after an earlier incident of laughter that Ford supervisors claimed slowed the production line by "maybe half a minute."[125]

Huxley's *Brave New World* draws upon Ford and Taylorism to the extent that the systematic dehumanization of workers at the Highland Park and Rouge factories in the twenties was a harrowing example of what Huxley regarded as the ruthlessness of the gifted. It was also a paradigmatic case of Russell's contention that power was the motivating factor in much of the modern application of scientific technique. Equally significant, the Ford system, like Taylor's, was inherently bureaucratic, in Weber's sense, and thus could serve as a model of the corporate state in *Brave New World*. Huxley never showed much understanding of or sympathy for the working class, but in his essays of the late twenties, he shared Russell's suspicions about the social consequences of modern technology and the desire for control and mastery of the scientific industrialist. The Director of Hatcheries exemplifies this dehumanizing embrace of Taylor-Ford mechanization that Huxley linked to the new romanticism, and that he so vividly depicted in the conveyor belt operations of the Director's laboratory.

In 1919 the Chicago Tribune referred to Henry Ford as an "ignorant idealist," for which Ford brought a suit for libel. During the ensuing trial, it became evident that Ford's knowledge was confined strictly to business, particularly after his responses on the stand to questions about American history. When a reporter asked him what he thought of history, he replied, "history is more or less the bunk. We want to live in the present, and the only history that is worth a tinker's damn is the history we make today."[126] In *Brave New World*, Mustapha Mond's first ideologically significant statement is a reaffirmation of Ford's revulsion for the past, what Mond calls " 'that beautiful and inspired saying of Our Ford's: History is bunk. History,' he repeated slowly, 'is bunk' " (38). "Our Ford," which of course rhymes with "Our Lord," is the secular deity of new romantic values and, as such, his biography is a key document in *Brave New World*, where it sits in a place of honor in Mustapha Mond's office.

Ford's anti-intellectualism was attacked by his contemporaries. André Siegfried, in *America Comes of Age* (1927), described what he called "Fordism" as an unbalanced celebration of automaton efficiency that threatened the basis of civilization. Garet Garrett's *Ouroborous, Or the Mechanical Extension of Mankind* (1925) focused on the delirious consumerism that both motivated and resulted from Ford's emphasis on mass production. R. M. Fox, in *The Triumphant Machine* (1928), derided Ford as an industrial plutocrat whose only reason for existence was to produce commodities in mindless profusion but who remained at bottom bored and dissatisfied with his instrumentalist philosophy. In *Behold America* (1931), S. D. Schmalhausen dismissed Ford as a "remarkable defective" best regarded as "the Mussolini of American Business." Ford himself contributed to this war of words in a series of books written with the aid of Samuel Crowther. His autobiography *My Life and Work* (1922) is essentially an apologia; it says little about Ford's personal life, focusing with relentless energy on a few simple ideas concerning industrial production and business affairs. In *Brave New World* this story of salvation through work and technology has supplanted the Bible. When, in chapter 16, John, the Savage, enters Mustapha Mond's study, he discovers lying on a table "a massive volume bound in limp black leather-surrogate and stamped with large golden T's. He picked it up and opened it. *My Life and Work, by Our Ford.* The book had been published at Detroit by the Society for the Propagation of Fordian Knowledge" (261).

Ford's autobiography is both an obvious and a subtle symbol of the hegemonic values of Mond's World State. On the simplest level it is the bible of mass production, the emblem of the Model T supplanting the Christian cross on its cover. But on a subtler level, the book celebrates the automobile, not the autobiographical self; it contains little personal information about Ford and thus it also reinforces the World State's aversion for personal identity, personal history, and any public references to personal experience. When, in chapter 6, Bernard Marx asks the Director of Hatcheries to initial his travel permit for a trip to the New Mexico Reservation, the latter begins to reminisce nostalgically about his own experiences there as a young man. Bernard's reaction is acute embarrassment. Shocked that the Director could "commit so gross a solecism," he wants "to hide his face, to run out of the room." By breaking the taboo against talking about the personal past and autobiographical facts, the Director had unintentionally done "the forbidden thing" (112), acknowledged a past and a self beyond the reach of the state. Ford's *My Life and Work* runs no such risk because the "life" is overwhelmed by the "work" and automotive themes displace autobiographical ones.

10

History and Psychology in the World State: Chapter 3

The opening chapters of *Brave New World* introduce the reader to a future inspired not only by "Our Ford" but by "Our Freud" as well. Huxley had always insisted that any assessment of the ideals animating western Euopean history after the First World War had to be based on "two tests, the historian's and the psychologist's."[127] In his social novels of the twenties Huxley made extensive use of Freudian ideas, populating his narratives with characters twisted and warped by neurosis and, occasionally, by psychotic fears and anxieties. Characters like Spandrell in *Point Counter Point* or Joseph Stoyte in *After Many a Summer Dies the Swan* were, in Huxley's view, socially representative types that exemplified the traits of a culture in decline. In his novels he drew upon Freudian psychoanalysis and "the Freudian 'complexes' for which family relationships are responsible."[128] In *Brave New World* he utilizes Freudian concepts in his characterization of John, the Savage, but in the introductory chapters the educational techniques of the World State are grounded in the behaviorist psychology of Ivan Pavlov and J. B. Watson discussed earlier.

Watson's application of the principles of mechanistic science to psychology led to a reduction of human behavior to the laws of phys-

History and Psychology in the World State

ics and chemistry. Such predictable and testable laws underlay Watson's psychology, which was premised on the belief that mind or consciousness was confined to physiological responses to external stimuli. Bertrand Russell, in *The Scientific Outlook*, regarded such an emphasis on the external stimulation of an essentially passive mind (i.e., conditioning) as a technique for acquiring power. Accordingly, the "menacing geniality" of the Director of Hatcheries suggests the peculiar combination of benign yet sinister coercion that informs all of the activities of the World State.

The introductory chapters describe a world in which the potentially refractory individual is socialized through behaviorist techniques of psychological conditioning. In chapter 2 the students are taken to the "Neo-Pavlovian Conditioning Rooms" where children are subjected to electric shocks and shrieking sirens in an effort to induce an "instinctive hatred of books and flowers" and in which the "reflexes" are "unalterably conditioned" (23). The final result of such "instruments of social stability" as behaviorist techniques is epitomized in the sleep teaching or "hypnopaedic" inculcation of "Elementary Class Consciousness" (30). Again, politics and science are merged as Huxley satirically conflates what in "The New Romanticism" he described as the Soviet communist's devotion to mechanistic science with what the Marxist finds most repulsive in capitalism, the class system. At the same time, Huxley invokes the capitalist's belief in Fordian mass production criticized in "The Outlook for American Culture" with the highly centralized bureaucracy characteristic of Soviet society. The result is a dystopian society combining what Huxley regarded as the most dangerous tendencies within the Soviet Union and the United States of the late twenties and early thirties—a combination of excessive reliance on technology and collectivist values resulting in a mechanized, rationalized society. Within such a state, Bernard's surname can be Marx and the woman he desires can be called Lenina, while both venerate the memory of "Our Ford."

The Central London Hatchery is not simply a symbol of a technology perverted to bad ends—the creation of a scientifically determined race of compliant automatons. Such a stifling of human possiblities as

89

a result of Pavlovian and Watsonian techniques is intrinsically political in that systematized behaviorist conditioning is a form of coercion set in motion by specialists in order to ensure social and political stability. The Director appeals to "high economic policy" as the ultimate justification of the World State's manipulative practices. The need to control the consumption of "manufactured articles" through the "socializing force" of genetic engineering, Taylorization, and behaviorist conditioning is one of the principal reasons for the existence of the Director's laboratories. His one moment of genuine excitement during his lecture occurs when, at the end, he suddenly exults, "But all these suggestions are *our* suggestions! . . . Suggestions from the State" (32). This assertion of the primacy of the state is an assertion about power and its sources, and leads to the appearance of "his fordship Mustapha Mond" at the beginning of the crucial third chapter.

The World State is governed by a committee. Mond is one of the ten World Controllers, and his appearance signals a shift in Huxley's use of psychology in *Brave New World*. Mond, like the Director, is a technical specialist, a scientist who fully endorses the behaviorist conditioning on which the security of the World State rests. In Mond's version of history, Freudian neurosis and destructively irrational or abnormal behavior are to be found only in what he calls the "terrible" past, before the introduction of universal conditioning techniques. In brief, Watsonian behaviorism is the stable, pacified present; Freudian psychosis was characteristic of human history before the establishment of Mond's utopia. The Savage, introduced later, who lives outside of the World State, is neurotic and irrationally violent for this reason; he lives in a precarious state of unconditioned freedom.

Mustapha Mond uses Freudian categories of thought solely in order to condemn the past. His very first words in *Brave New World* compose a sweeping repudiation of the past, in particular, its inability to come to terms with human sexuality and erotic desire. Just before Mond's appearance, the Director and his students, having completed their tour of the Hatchery, walk outside to observe the games of the children—including "erotic play." The Director uses the occasion to muse on history, warning his students that "when you're not accustomed to history, most facts about the past *do* sound incredible" (36). The incredible fact that he proceeds to reveal is that erotic play between children was once regarded as abnormal. As his students gape in disbelief and ask what the results were, Mustapha Mond appears for the first time and announces, "The results were terrible" (37).

Mond's verdict on nonutopian history introduces the historical summary characteristic of the modern dystopia. In the main section of chapter 3, subdivided into 123 smaller units, Huxley contrasts the stable behaviorist present of the World State with its unstable neurotic past by means of an assortment of voices. Throughout this section the voice of the anonymous third person narrator is supplemented by the voices of major characters like Bernard Marx and Lenina Crowne, and minor figures like Henry Foster and Fanny. The result is a medley of social perspectives that collectively express the social texture of World State society. As the chapter proceeds, however, the reader becomes aware of the increasingly dominant voice of the World Controller, Mustapha Mond. When collated, Mond's observations can be seen to compose a fragmented but sufficiently continuous record of history prior to the establishment of his scientific utopia. Equally important—and illustrative of Huxley's belief in the close interrelationship between psychology and history—Mond's remarks are inspired by a discussion of sexuality, erotic desire, and the nuclear family as a social institution.

Like Gibbon in his *Decline and Fall of the Roman Empire,* Mond views history as "little more than the register of the crimes, follies, and misfortunes of mankind." He simply discards world history from the ancient Middle East ("Harappa . . . Ur of the Chaldees . . . Thebes and Babylon and Cnossos and Mycenae") up to "the pre-moderns," just prior to the founding of the World State. He rejects everything, including literature, music, art, and philosophy. For Mond, the World State is a state without a past, continuous with nothing beyond itself. Preutopian history he interprets as a turbulent record of violence, pathology, and irrational excess. "That's why you're taught no history," he informs the students. But, like the Director, he immediately contradicts himself, adding, "but now the time has come" for a history lesson.

The Director is surprised at Mond's willingness to raise the forbidden subject, and remembers the "strange rumours of old forbidden books hidden in a safe in the Controller's study" (39). Like many of the inhabitants of the World State, Mond cannot completely control his fascination with time and history. He begins his lecture of fallen or pre-utopian mankind with, in his view, the quintessential Eve, "a viviparous mother" (40), that is, a symbol of natural childbearing. The family and its basis in maternity have been rendered obsolete by World State technology. They have been banished as a source of economic as well as psychological instability. Mond defines the family as the creation of the mother, a site of aberrancy and disease "as squalid psychically as physically." The home of premodern times he describes as "an understerilized prison" (42), an airless rabbit hole, "hot with the frictions of tightly packed life, reeking with emotion. What suffocating intimacies, what dangerous, insane, obscene relationships between the members of the family group" (42). At the center stands the mother, "maniacally" infecting her children with "every kind of perversion from sadism to chastity" (44). Mond's disgust with familial relationships can be traced to the Freudian assessment of the family and what Huxley called, as noted earlier, those "Freudian 'complexes' for which family relationships are responsible." The reference to sadism and chastity is important because the Savage, as we shall see, suffers from a sadistic obsession with sexual chastity as a result of his mother's influence.

Mond loathes the image of the mother, and while he inveighs against it as a source of incapacitating neurosis, the voice of Lenina Crowne appears in the text for the first time. Lenina is the new woman, sexually promiscuous, free of family responsibilities, and conditioned to feel only aversion for monogamous relationships. Her first remarks are part of a discussion with her friend Fanny on the advisability of a Pregnancy Substitute; but the conversation shifts to Lenina's perplexing tendency to see the same man for extended periods of time.

History and Psychology in the World State

In a society where undiscriminating promiscuity is a virtue, Lenina's preference for long-drawn-out affairs with only one male is regarded as perversely immoral. While Fanny warns Lenina about her antisocial behavior, Mustapha Mond continues his attack on "mother, monogamy, [and] romance" (47), arguing that such a stress on loyalty and romantic love fostered neurosis and "endless isolating pain." What Mond fears in monogamous love is its intensity of feeling, because such emotional energy encouraged the "instability" of individualism. This is the all-important thematic point in Mond's diatribes against romantic love and the family; he fears the sense of individual identity fed and nurtured by subjective feelings.

Mond's repudiation of strong or concentrated feeling is linked to the essential ideological principle on which the World State is founded. For the World Controller, history is a record of abnormal pathology, an immense case history of neurotic and psychotic behavior. Society is a patient who must be tranquilized, calmed, rendered passive and stable, hence the mass distributions of the drug *soma*. Mond identifies stability as "the primal and ultimate need" (44), defining it as a state of "calm well-being." The reason he regards the family as a threat to such placid contentedness lies in his distinctly Freudian preoccupation with the violent consequences of frustrated desire and repression. The family is indicted as the scene of destabilizing impulses born of repressed desires, irrationally intense emotion, and egocentric rivalry. The resulting Freudian complexes are to be laid to rest by means of behaviorist conditioning. These two irreconcilable psychologies are brought together in *Brave New World* in such a way that one provides the diagnosis, the other, the cure.

In Huxley's view Freudian depth psychology turned on the pivotal concept of covert or unconscious mental activity, especially the idea of unconscious desire that could be repressed and thus become productive of inner turmoil and irrational behavior. Within Mustapha Mond's world of conditioned serenity and social stability, the single enemy is arrested desire, symbolized by the decanted infant howling for his bottle. What Mond and his bureaucratic technicians fear is the irrational intensity of raw desiring emotion. "Feeling lurks in that interval of time between desire and its consummation" (51), Mond says, and he is dedicated to obliterating the moment of unsatisfied desire. The World State is, after all, utopia. By removing the moment of unconsummated desire, Mond will eliminate intense emotion itself, because strong emotion is born of frustrated desire. By disposing of vital emotion he will have extinguished selfhood or personal identity, thus ensuring both personal and social stability.

In the interwar period the key texts for such an anxious perspective on human behavior in relation to history and society were Freud's *Civilization and its Discontents* and *The Future of an Illusion*. Freud's philosophy of history was a relatively somber one, stressing the irrational intensity of human desires and appetites and the resulting need for coercion, for the renunciation of instinctual desire and its sublimation in creative work. Religion he dismissed as a mass delusion, arguing that it had to be supplanted by science. The limited degree of progress open to humanity was dependent on humanity's capacity for collective self-discipline, especially the renunciation of the more powerful and hence more destructive forms of erotic desire. Such a process of disciplined control could be achieved by means of sublimation, that is, the modification, deflection, and taming of appetitive energies by channeling them into socially acceptable and stabilizing forms of activity (i.e., art, science, technology, etc.). Accordingly, the goal of history was the establishment of scientific consciousness in the manner of H. G. Wells's *Men Like Gods*. The intellectual ascendancy of the scientific state of mind would control and harness humanity's more irrational psychological drives, and that, in turn, could lead to control of both the social and natural environment. But Freud also believed that utopia was a dream; the barbaric past and the destructive psychic impulses that energized it are always present, always a potential threat to social and individual harmony. Mustapha Mond's World State is premised on this darker view of human potentiality in which Wells's scientific rationalist like the Utopian Urthred is always in danger of succumbing to the "ancestral man-ape" within.

In his lecture to the Director's students Mond employs the simple metaphor of water under pressure to illustrate his understanding of the dynamics of human desire, observing that the more holes are punched in a water pipe, the weaker the pressure of each individual leak. Mond's answer to destructively intense desire is to let off the pressure wherever possible, in systematically controlled ways. His view of civilization is essentially permissive, especially in the sphere of sexuality. Sexual promiscuity is held up as a normal human activity; indeed, he regards it as a socially beneficial mode of behavior in a society where sensual appetite is pandered to in a scientifically coordinated way. Mond promises the reduction of the "interval of time between desire and its consummation" through the universal availability of the objects of desire. To do this on a large scale, the objects are commodified; the women of his utopia are sexual objects—as are the men—in a society "where every one belongs to every one else." What appetites remain are neutralized by drugs and sophisticated forms of entertainment, like the Feelies. What is absent in the World State is any form of self-denial, especially the sublimation or deflection of appetitive energy into the creation of art, literature, music, or genuinely creative science. Such activities would require the deferral or renunciation of sensual desire, and Mond fears such repression as productive of neurosis and violent emotion. "Impulse arrested," he warns the students, "spills over, and the flood is feeling, the flood is passion, the flood is even madness: it depends on the force of the current, the height and strength of the barrier. The unchecked stream flows smoothly down its appointed channels into a calm well-being" (50). The government of the World State clearly prefers the "unchecked stream" of satisfied desire and its resulting social order of hedonistic conformity.

Mond's summary of "pre-modern history," then, is history viewed as a case record of pathological violence born of socially uncoordinated energies. In the "new era" such anarchic impulses are not rechanneled into art or scientific research but simply damped down by means of drugs or placated by an ethic of immediate satisfaction. The past is terrible because unstable. Human civilization, informed by neurotic aims and ambitions, may have produced the paintings of Michelangelo and the plays of Shakespeare, but at too high a price. As the Fordian apologist for the "interests of industry" and the Freudian advocate of the pleasure principle, Mond emphasizes only the disruptive and anarchic aspects of history. He has no faith in humanity's capacity for self-disciplined and creative labor, and this pessimism is reflected in his history of the "pre-modern" era. As in Wells's *The Sleeper Awakes* or Zamiatin's *We*, the period of history prior to the establishment of utopia is one of increasing civil violence and widespread social instability. Mond's chronology can be collated as follows:

A.F. 1 (1908)	The opening date of the new era. The introduction of Our Ford's first Model T (1908). Period of liberalism and the appearance of "the first reformers."
A.F. 141 (2049)	Outbreak of "The Nine Years' War" followed by "the great Economic Collapse." Period of Russian ecological warfare including the poisoning of rivers and the anthrax bombing of Germany and France.
A.F. 150 (2058)	The beginning of "World Control." The "conscription of consumption" followed by a period of social restiveness and instability. The rise of "Conscientious objection and [a] back to nature movement." The reaction to liberal protest movements including the Golders Green massacre of "Simple Lifers" and the British Museum Massacre. Abandonment of force by the World Controllers. Period of an antihistory movement and social reeducation including intensive propaganda directed against viviparous reproduction and a "campaign against the Past." Closing of museums. Suppression of all books published before A.F. 150.
A.F. 178 (2086)	Government drive to discover a socially useful narcotic without damaging side effects. Establishment of special programs in pharmacology and biochemistry.
A.F. 184 (2092)	The discovery of *soma*.
A.F. 473 (2381)	The Cyprus Experiment: establishment of a wholly Alpha community.
A.F. 478 (2386)	Civil War in Cyprus. Nineteen thousand Alphas killed.

History and Psychology in the World State

A.F. 482   The Ireland Experiment (increased leisure time and four-hour
(2390)   work week).

A.F. 632   The present of *Brave New World.*
(2540)

Mond's chronicle of the foundation of the new era highlights two aspects of World State ideology. First, it stresses the attempt to obliterate all knowledge of the past, the antihistory movement reflecting the new era's need to seize control of the historical record, not to rewrite it, as in Orwell's *Nineteen Eighty-Four,* but to remove the concept of history itself from human consciousness. Second, in the references to the "back to nature movement" and the emphasis on technological experimentation, it foregrounds the typical dystopian opposition between nature and reason. Equally important, Mond's chronicle does not suggest a progressive unfolding of human potentiality (as in Wells's *Men Like Gods*). The final social experiments in Cyprus and Ireland are indicative of human limits, of boundaries beyond which humanity cannot develop. The World State is not the beginning of a new period of evolving and progressing civilization that Wells had celebrated in *Men Like Gods.* Rather, it is a massive socioeconomic improvisation marking the final termination of history. It is premised on the futility of history and offers in its stead what amounts to the apocalyptic ushering in of a society so authoritarian and immobile that historical progress has been halted, rather like a river frozen in its bed. This achievement of, in Mond's words, "the stablest equilibrium in history" (272) is attributable to a paralysis of historical process that extends to the temporal experience of the individual citizen, where birth most often leads to arrested development, and where life involves a mindless dedication to the immediate present. Neither past nor future has meaning.

Mond's chronicle, with its emphasis on the linear, sequential nature of time and the irrationality of past history, brings into sharper focus the principal anxiety of the World State: the disruptive nature of time itself. It is not just the cultural past and the study of history that is banished from Mond's dystopia. Temporal process is regarded as a condition to be carefully calibrated and controlled. The hypnopaedic sentence, "Ending is better than mending," that is whispered into the ears of sleeping children at the Hatchery is typical in this respect. The statement is an economic principle that encourages commodity consumption rather than a more frugal concern with wasteful and unnecessary expenditure. But "ending" is also a temporal concept suggesting the principal aim of World State ideology: the ending of desire in immediate satisfaction, the ending of history in the new era where future progress ("mending") is irrelevant.

Mond's "now" of the World State involves a complete immersion in present time. If desire is deferred then dissatisfaction persists in time with—as Mond believes—all of its attendant frustrations and unstable emotions. "Now," he proclaims "the old men work, the old men copulate, the old men *have no time,* no leisure from pleasure, *not a moment* to sit down and think" (66–67; emphasis added). The final escape from time is the drug *soma,* defined by Mond as "a dark eternity," that is, as inducing an inherently timeless state of mind. What Mond fears is the appearance of "a crevice of time," unexpectedly yawning "in the solid substance" of World State materialism (67). He asks his audience, "Has any of you been compelled to live through a long time-interval between the consciousness of a desire and its fulfillment?" (52). Such an interval or "crevice of time" is a space in which the mind can expand and develop, in which desire can be rechanneled or sublimated. It is also a site of disruptive emotion or longing. Bernard Marx is viewed with suspicion by Fanny because "he spends most of his time by himself" (52).

The endeavor of the technocrats "to conquer old age" (65) is part of a wider, more subtle agenda that would force humanity to alter profoundly its experience of time. The World State, then, is, in a manner of speaking, a new time zone where characters remain constant throughout a whole lifetime, where the stages of birth, maturity, and aging no longer have meaning, and where historical process has simply ended. It is, accordingly, appropriate that the collage of voices composing chapter 3, including Mond's dominant voice, should end with the novel's presiding symbol of the World State's technological dominance of time: "Slowly, majestically, with a faint humming of machinery, the Conveyors moved forward, thirty-three centimeters an hour" (67). This final image of the conquest of natural childbirth is also a symbol of the victory over natural time—or at least what can be called the unmanipulated temporal experience characteristic of the pre-modern age so thoroughly condemned by Mond. Bernard Marx is introduced to the reader as an error in World State calibrations, someone for whom the "interval of time between desire and its consummation" is continually widening. Out of step with his fellow citizens, he threatens to disrupt the stately movement of the Fordian production line with distinctly Freudian disturbances.

11

Time, Love, and Bernard Marx:
Chapters 4–6

Huxley's *Brave New World*, like Zamiatin's *We* and Orwell's *Nineteen Eighty-Four*, organizes its various political and historical themes around a love affair—in the case of *Brave New World*, around two love affairs. All three writers have, for obvious reasons, placed a personal and private relationship at the center of their narratives about impersonal and oppressively public societies. In a dehumanizing, obsessively rational, and inherently loveless state, the emotional intensity of romantic relationships takes on a distinctly radical cast. Huxley, however, has created a series of romantic entanglements so perversely abnormal and self-destructive as to undermine any hope of an alternative to Mond's collectivist ideology. Bernard Marx, the narrative's nominal hero, makes his first appearance in chapter 3, primarily as an object of gossip and derision. Despite his rank as an Alpha Plus, Bernard has a bad reputation among his fellow workers, principally as a consequence of his desire for privacy. Undersized and physically unattractive, he is overwhelmed by feelings of inadequacy as well as hatred for the more conventionally endowed and culturally assimilated people around him. In a society where "every one belongs to every one else" (50), Bernard has unaccountably developed monogamous impulses. Like Lenina, who, despite her hypnopaedic conditioning, tends to remain with one man for longer than society deems acceptable, Bernard has experienced the first stirrings of romantic desire, and he has become infatuated with her. Their relationship fails to develop, however, just as neither character is capable of significant intellectual or spiritual growth. Bernard is quickly overshadowed by the more richly conceived Savage, while Lenina, whose monogamous tendencies suggest that the World State's control of its citizens is less than absolute, remains a mere focal point for each man's perceptions of what he desires. Bernard, despite his hatred for World State society and his confused need to experience something new, especially something primitive and natural, remains a prisoner of his psychological conditioning.

Bernard's attraction to Lenina, however, is both romantic and ideological to the extent that it opposes itself to two fundamental World State values. He objects to the socioeconomic role that Lenina is forced to play within the erotic economy of Mond's utopia. Specifically, he objects to the gross promiscuity of his fellow citizens. His admission that he hates them takes place in a specifically erotic context. Overhearing a conversation between Henry Foster and the Assistant Predestinator about Lenina's sexual skills in which Foster passes her on with an enthusiastic recommendation to the Assistant Predestinator, Bernard turns pale with outrage: "Talking about her as though she were a bit of meat. . . . Have her here, have her there. Like mutton. Degrading her to so much mutton" (53). Later, he adds, "and what makes it worse, she thinks of herself as meat" (63). His fierce reaction to the degradation of women in the World State is ideological as well as emotional or merely romantic. Mond's society is founded on the concept of the "goods-consuming citizen" (283), that is, on carefully regulated overconsumption and materialism. Put as simply as possible, Lenina is a genetically designed commodity for erotic consumption. In first defining his interest in Lenina in the context of materialist sensuality and commodity consumerism, Bernard has linked his emotional attraction to Lenina to the basic values of his society. To that somewhat inchoate degree, it is a political act.

Huxley underscores the ideological dimension of their affair with

BRAVE NEW WORLD

its potential for social and personal disruption by having it consist of
two trips, both beyond the comforting familiarities of the essentially
urban World State. The journeys—the first, a brief flight over the sea
in order to experience the stormy and alien aspect of nature, and the
second, to the New Mexico Reservation in order to confront the primitive past—are both symbolic attempts to contact what can no longer
be experienced, much less comprehended, by the utopian technocrat.
Both excursions end in failure because they both involve what for
Bernard and Lenina are impassable barriers, the first in space and the
second in time.

   In his dramatization of Bernard Marx's discreetly apathetic rebellion against the confining pleasure of utopia, Huxley reinforces his
symbolic role by making him the embodiment of Mond's greatest
fear, unsatisfied desire. As noted earlier, it is "the interval of time
between desire and its consummation" that Mond fears because it
creates emotion and self-consciousness. The World State is intent on
drowning self-consciousness by means of an immersion in a present
of completely satisfied desire. Bernard encapsulates this theme with
particular clarity when he complains of a desire that can never be
pacified: " 'I am I, and wish I wasn't'; his self-consciousness was
acute and distressing" (76). This troubled confession of frustrated
desire and its resulting sense of heightened personal identity is crucial
for the reader's comprehension of Bernard's thematic role. He is the
quintessential outsider. As an object of others' derision, his experience of "being slighted and alone" feeds directly into his increasing
awareness of individual autonomy. But his often-voiced opposition to
the mindless consumerism of the World State is rooted less in conscious political opposition than in feelings of physical inadequacy
attributable to his short stature ("eight centimeters short of the standard Alpha height"). Bernard wants to be standard, but he also
opposes the standard treatment of Lenina by other male Alphas and
Betas. Similarly, he seeks out opportunities to be alone, yet he also
resents his exclusion from society. This inner conflict of frustrated
conformist desires and rebellious impulses has sharpened his sense of

individuality. Nevertheless, he remains, despite his ambivalent actions, a product of his coercive culture.

His first journey beyond the confines of such coercion is the helicopter trip with Lenina described in chapter 5. The theme of time is raised again when Lenina proposes an afternoon at a country club followed by dinner. Bernard characteristically objects to crowds and dismisses her suggestions of golf as "a waste of time." She responds with the novel's fundamental question: "Then what's time for?" (104). Everything in *Brave New World* revolves around Lenina's query. Bernard's answer is simply going for "walks in the Lake District," a response that involves more than nature and unregulated activity. The Lake District in England was intimately associated with the British romantic poets Wordsworth and Coleridge. Huxley defined modern romanticism with its celebration of machinery, technology, and "Collective Man" as a false utopian vision of the "Bolshevik millennium": "To the Bolshevik idealist, Utopia is indistinguishable from one of Mr. Henry Ford's factories."[129] The old romanticism of Shelley or Wordsworth, however, was liberal in its espousal of individualism. Bernard's choice of the Lake district, of privacy and conversation, is a political choice to the extent that it endorses what Huxley viewed as the liberal values of romantics like Shelley and Godwin. Bored at such a prospect, Lenina dashes Bernard's hopes by insisting on a more substantial way of filling the time, persuading him to take her to the Women's Heavyweight Wrestling Championship in Amsterdam. On the return trip, over the English Channel at night, Bernard takes his revenge.

Slowing the helicopter, he descends to within a hundred feet of the waves. At the same time, the sky clouds over and a strong wind springs up. Lenina suddenly finds herself beyond the ordered and enclosed space of utopia, in what she calls a "horrible place" consisting of emptiness and flux: "She was appalled by the rushing emptiness of the night, by the black foam-flecked water heaving beneath them, by the pale face of the moon, so haggard and distracted among the hastening clouds" (105–6). The empty, stormy sea is the first intrusion of nature into the text of *Brave New World*. Such a fluid and changing scene is the antitype of World State stability. Its "rushing emptiness" is a variation on the theme of the "crevice of time" that Mustapha Mond fears will suddenly "yawn in the solid substance" of World State routine. To Lenina's consternation, Bernard confesses that the stormy void below them reinforces his sense of self, claiming that it "makes me feel as though . . . I were more *me*, if you see what I mean. . . . Not just a cell in the social body" (106).

In *Proper Studies* Huxley observed that he found "incomprehensible the state of mind of those to whom the flux of reality seems something dreadful and repulsive. Enjoying my bath in the flux, I feel no longing for rocks of ages or other similar eternal solidities. I am in my element in the current, and pant for no dry land."[130] Lenina, fearful of the natural scene below her, does pant for dry land, that is, for the solid, time-filling distractions of Mond's urban utopia. As a result, Bernard is forced to return to England and participate in the obligatory sex that Lenina has been conditioned to expect. Reversing conventional roles, he thinks to himself that "she doesn't mind being meat," and even complains that he didn't want their trip to end with their "going to bed" (109).

Though the excursion to Amsterdam with its unexpected deviation over the Channel ends in failure, Bernard is undeterred and immediately arranges for a second, more ambitious trip. The theme of time reemerges as Bernard speculates on whether "it might be possible to be an adult all the time" (110). He hopes to answer this radical conjecture by means of a journey into the racial past. In his conversation with the Director of Hatcheries, whose permission is necessary for the New Mexico excursion, he is surprised at the Director's sudden violation of social propriety. The Director confesses to Bernard that he once had the same idea and begins to reminisce about the remote past. The conjunction of individual memory and the proposed journey to the primitive past of the New Mexico Reservation is significant in that both areas are forbidden; that is, they are ideologically beyond the boundaries of utopia. The Director's memories are of loss and unsatisfied desire. On his trip he was separated from his companion, a young woman who wandered off alone and got lost in a thunderstorm. She was never found, but the Director confesses that he still dreams about "being woken up by that peal of thunder and finding her gone . . . of seaching and searching for her under the trees" (114). Normally able to repress his unconsummated desire, the Director falls into this crevice of time during his sleep—an admission that should interest Bernard but, for the most part, merely provokes conventional embarrassment, as conventional as Lenina's earlier responses to his own desire to walk alone in the Lake District. Nevertheless, Bernard will discover the Director's long-lost companion on the New Mexico Reservation and restore her to utopia.

Bernard's expedition to the New Mexico Reservation is an uncomprehending journey into the cultural past that culminates not in a deeper apprehension of who and what he is, but rather in his displacement by the ostensibly more authentic voice of the Savage. Bernard is uneducable, and his flickering perceptions of something deeper and finer than the organized apathy of World State culture never develop. He never grows into his desired perpetual adulthood and, by the end of the novel, actually regresses. The high point of his psychological and political development occurs when, after he is sharply criticized by the Director for his antisocial behavior, he experiences a sense of intensified selfhood: "He stood alone, embattled against the order of things; elated by the intoxicating consciousness of his individual significance and importance" (115). After his climactic encounter with the Savage, he slips back into the euphoric present of the World State and its collectivist ideology.

12

Huxley's Retrospective Utopia and the Role of the Savage: Chapter 7

Bernard's journey to the Savage Reservation is, at least on the surface, a return to a state of nature that will be counterpointed by the Savage's reverse journey from the anthropological past to the utopian future. Both journeys are presumably educative and both are motivated, at least in part, by an attraction to Lenina Crowne. Bernard and the Savage, however, share more than their involvement with Lenina; they are mirror images of each other. Bernard is the new romantic struggling to transcend collectivist and technological values. The Savage, a product of a society mired in superstition and ignorance, is, paradoxically, a lover of art and Shakespeare. Intent upon a life of individual self-expression and freedom, he functions thematically as the representative of Huxley's old romantic liberalism.

As psychological opposites who confront each other across the electric fence of the Reservation, they can be best understood in terms of the imagery Huxley used in "The New Romanticism," especially his metaphor of the photographic negative: "Modern romanticism is the old romanticism turned inside out, with all its values reversed. Their plus is the modern minus; the modern good is the old bad. What then was black is now white, what was white is now black. Our romanticism is the photographic negative of that which flourished during the corresponding years of [the] last century."[131] Bernard and the Savage are reversed cultural types. Bernard is the dark negative, his shadowy life linked to collective and technocratic values. The Savage is the bright developed image of old romantic individualism, and natural as opposed to mechanistic principles of explanation and belief. However, this clear opposition is complicated by Bernard's emergent opposition to World State technology and by the Savage's neurotic behavior and fanatical idealism. Bernard, never fully comprehending his own motives, is hoping for guidance from the Savage, while the Savage is too mentally unbalanced to offer a clear alternative that might permit Bernard to escape the impasse in which he finds himself.

Both men have been psychologically crippled by their childhood experiences within their very different cultures. Bernard is the product of the behaviorist conditioning techniques of Pavlov and Watson and yet is not completely conditioned. The Savage, however, is more complex. Free of the coercive educative policies of the World State, he ought to function as the healthy natural and unrestrained alternative to the repressed Bernard. In the dystopian narratives of Zamiatin and Orwell, this basic generic opposition is preserved. There, the artificial technocracies of an ostensible utopia are contrasted with a free, liberated space populated by individuals living in a natural setting—a setting, moreover, associated with sexuality, love, and passion. In *Brave New World* Huxley has significantly altered this generic code to the extent of creating the major interpretive problem of his novel. As observed earlier, Wells established the basic generic features of the twentieth-century utopia. Zamiatin reversed them in his dystopia, *We.* Huxley continued this approach but complicated it by means of his problematic treatment of the Indian reservation and its ambiguous primitive, John, the Savage. In *Brave New World* the alternative to Mond's new era of scientific totalitarianism appears to be equally unattractive. Both Bernard and the Savage are social outsiders. As marginalized figures they find themselves unable to participate in the life of their communities. One is too short, the other too white. Both are troubled by women. Each is critical of the presiding ideology of his respective society and, as a result, is viewed with contempt by those around him. Both desire Lenina Crowne. Their principal point of contrast is that the Savage can deal with time; that is, he can compose an autobiography and narrate his life story. This is an attempt at self-understanding well in advance of Bernard, who struggles to understand himself but who has no family past and thus no story to tell. Instead, he listens to the Savage compose a narrative out of his own family and individual experiences in the hope of learning something about what it means to grow, develop, and finally "be an adult all the time." The problem, however, is that the Savage's autobiography is a Freudian case study of childhood neurosis.

The journey to the Reservation reintroduces the motif of time when Lenina praises the efficient "schedule time" of the Blue Pacific Rocket (117). Like the conveyor belts at the Hatchery where she works, the movement of the rocket involves carefully calibrated linear sequence. In the mindless present of the World State, time is perceived only in the context of technological function, which aims at reducing the interval between desire and the satisfaction of desire. Lenina, however, is moving into the primitive past, a radical shift in time perception that will require a more imaginative response than she and Bernard are used to making. When they arrive at the Reservation, they first encounter the Warden, who recites a prepared lecture on the features of the Reservation. Not unexpectedly, he sees it in terms of numbers relating to size, population, and power requirements. Bernard's introduction to primitive New Mexico begins inauspiciously with a preoccupation with World State time. As the Warden drones on, Bernard remembers that he had left the cologne tap in his bathroom turned on and anxiously envisions the needle on the scent meter creeping round and round, raising his bill. This seemingly trivial incident involves the major theme of the central chapters of *Brave New World*. The experience of the Reservation will involve both historical and biographical memory. The culture that Bernard will confront is part of the racial past, just as the Savage's autobiography will be rooted in his personal past. To even begin to understand either requires some knowledge of social and cultural history or some knowledge of what it means to have a personal history. Bernard has neither, because the World State has transformed him into a kind of amnesiac. Forbidden to study history and denied authentic identity with its roots extending back into past experience (including a family), he suffers from a form of cultural amnesia. Thus, his first act of remembering when he arrives at the Reservation is a symbolic one. It combines materialism (loss of money), the technological perception of time as simple measurement (the dial needle), and triviality, the image of the flowing faucet with its black needle "nibbling through time, eating into his money" (120). Calling Helmholtz Watson (and noting that it takes nearly three minutes), he learns that the Director of Hatcheries has decided, during his absence, to assign Bernard to Iceland. Bernard, horrified at this prospect, collapses. Lenina offers him *soma* in an image that symbolically encapsulates his dilemma: "In the end she persuaded him to swallow four tablets of *soma*. Five minutes later roots and fruits were abolished; the flower of the present rosily blossomed" (123). Past time (roots) and future (fruits) are extinguished in a timeless, drug-induced present. True to his utopian origins, Bernard, despite his radical impulses, remains a thoroughly conditioned citizen of Mond's World State.

The importance of this brief episode, placed at the beginning of the central events of the narrative, is further reinforced by a second memory of much greater significance than the running faucet. Bernard suddenly recalls his earlier desire for suffering, for some kind of painful trial that would augment his sense of selfhood. This second memory will establish his principal connection with the Savage: "Often in the past he had wondered what it would be like to be subjected (*soma*-less and with nothing but his own inward resources to rely on) to some great trial, some pain, some persecution; he had even longed for affliction" (122). His desire for a kind of ordeal is inseparable from the theme of time because it is in the "interval of time," the crevice or gap between desire and its fulfillment, that the self presumably grows and develops. Huxley is suggesting that self-denial and self-realization are subtly linked. Lenina's pivotal question—"Then what's time for?"— has an answer waiting in the Reservation, but in an alien and enigmatic form that will test her and Bernard's imaginative powers.

In order to reach the pueblo in the valley of Malpais, Bernard and Lenina cross a symbolic line of demarcation separating "civilization from savagery." Flying over the desert they see below them a seemingly endless electrified fence that marches "on and on, irresistibly the straight line, the geometrical symbol of triumphant human purpose" (123). As a line of mathematical purity, the fence symbolizes the lethality of World State rationalism when confronted with natural processes. The fence is a weapon; its function is to divide by killing. Surrounded by the electrocuted carcasses and bones of dead animals, it emblematizes the domination of nature by utopian technology. In its starkness of opposition it also alludes to the generic convention of reason versus nature in the utopian novels of Wells and Zamiatin. In one of the novel's most ironic moments, the pilot of the aircraft laughs at the animal skeletons that lie scattered beside the fence, observing that "they never learn. . . . And they never will learn." His sense of having "scored a personal triumph over the electrocuted animals" (124) is ironic in that his own life has been determined by behaviorist conditioning techniques, including the use of electricity (for example, the electric shock therapy employed in the Hatchery to condition the reflexes of the children). The capacity to learn from experience is fundamental to culture and civilization, but all Huxley's pilot has demonstrated is a passive capacity to be manipulated by means of stimulus-response conditioning.

The pilot's misplaced sense of superiority introduces the central issue addressed in the chapters that follow, the problem of nature and its relationship to Mond's technocracy. In "History and the Past" Huxley warned about distorted evaluations of primitive societies, observing that "with every advance of industrial civilization the savage past will be more and more appreciated, and the cult of D. H. Lawrence's *Dark God* may be expected to spread through an ever-widening circle of worshippers."[132] Huxley's depiction of the culture of Malpais rests on a primary assumption of his philosophy of history, that historical reconstructions of the past are often as ideologically distorted as historical projections of the future. Accordingly, he was as increasingly impatient with "the primitive and prehistoric Utopias of D. H. Lawrence" as he was with the future utopias of H. G. Wells. In Lawrence's novels, especially *The Rainbow* and *Women in Love,* he juxtaposed the industrial whir and clatter of mechanized civilization with what he regarded as more authentic levels of being. Lawrence placed great stress on the artificiality of the overly rationalized, excessively cerebral nature of modern civilization. In its stead he endorsed what he claimed to be the regenerative powers of deeply passional states of feeling, including erotic experience. His celebration of the immediate experiences of nature as profoundly restorative of a deeper sensual identity beyond the reach of rational or intellectual modes of perception influenced Huxley's work during the late twenties, particularly the essays of *Do What You Will* and his finest novel, *Point Counter Point.* Lawrence's attack on the dehumanizing power of industrialized European culture took the form of a sustained exploration of alternative ways of returning to states of passional spontaneity and of some kind of harmonious reconciliation of spirit and flesh, male and female, intellect and nature. He viewed Western civilization as decaying from within and attempted, with declining success, to envision its utopian replacement. Huxley, always sympathetic to theories of historical decline, found in Lawrence a complexly suggestive diagnosis of contemporary society. Like Lawrence, Huxley tended to see history in terms of cyclical patterns and was profoundly wary of industrialized and bureaucratized technocracy. Also, like Lawrence, Huxley tended to interpret history according to psychological frames of reference. Huxley's interest in Lawrence reaches into *Point Counter Point,* where he created Mark Rampion, a character based on his personal knowledge of Lawrence and, with some modification, his understanding of Lawrence's ideas about modern history. Thus Rampion insists that "social collapse . . . results from psychological collapse," and that modern industrial progress had led to a "psychological impasse" in which human nature had become excessively cerebral and overly rationalized.[133] The atrophy of more natural instincts and psychological states had resulted in a culture that Lawrence (like Huxley) depicted as self-divided and suicidal.

While Huxley sympathized with Lawrence's diagnosis of modern culture, he did not accept his cure. Lawrence's solution to the coercive and deformative aspects of modern technocratic societies struck Huxley as the vision of a "retrospective Utopist" whose formulations, at least in relation to primitive levels of being, were both false and inherently ideological. The retrospective Utopist, he argued, creates a "wish-fulfilling world" rooted in "contemporary politico-economic ideals." In "History and the Past" Huxley reviewed the various idealized visions of the past, from medieval to classical Greek, where each Utopist discovers "his own snug little Utopia, feudal, Socialist, or Catholic." Huxley objected to Lawrence's primitivism as merely a further development of the attempt to envision "a pre-mechanical world" that preoccupied a number of nineteenth-century writers like William Morris or, later, G. K. Chesterton and Hillaire Belloc. Their medieval utopias, he argued, had been displaced in modern literature by "the savages—not even noble ones now; we almost prefer them ignoble." This endeavor to discover "the fully and harmoniously developed individual man" within a past culture, whether medieval craftsman, classical Greek, or primitive savage, was open to the same objections Huxley leveled against H. G. Wells's Utopian of the future. They were "compensatory" evasions of contemporary problems, oversimplified and distorted.[134]

Brave New World attempts to expose the fallacies of both the technological utopist, with his vision of a gleaming future world state, and "the retrospective Utopist" who idealizes the past even to the point of embracing "the comfortable darkness beyond the fringes of recorded history."[135] Lawrence had celebrated such a return to primeval "race-experiences" during his trips to New Mexico. Huxley had talked with him about his responses to Mexico, and Lawrence published several brief essays about Indian culture, including one entitled "The Hopi Snake Dance." However, Peter Firchow notes that much of Huxley's knowledge of the customs of the Pueblo Indians can be traced to Frank Cushing's *Zuni Folk Tales* (1901) and, on Huxley's own admission, to the studies of Pueblo Indian culture published in the *Annual Report of the Bureau of Ethnology.*[136]

The New Mexico chapters are much more, however, than a critique of D. H. Lawrence's primitivist utopia. This section of *Brave New World* raises the central issue of the modern dystopia, the opposition between science and nature, and its embodiment in two contrasting societies. Moreover, Huxley radically alters this generic convention by not permitting his reader the luxury of a simple opposition, expected and easy to comprehend. Instead, the anticipated antagonism between analytic reason and natural instinct involves more ambiguous, less easily pigeonholed sets of ideas. The opposition between science and nature is emphasized, but the critical issue turns on whether nature offers a viable alternative to an already discredited technocracy. The first hint we get of this is the name of the New Mexico pueblo community, "Malpais." In Spanish this means "bad place" or "bad country," and hence the term seems identical to "dystopia" ("bad place" in Greek). But Mustapha Mond's World State has already been satirized as a dystopia masking as a utopian paradise. The answer to this dilemma is to be found in the character of the Savage and the autobiographical story he tells to Bernard.

When Bernard and Lenina arrive at Malpais, they first encounter an Indian disabled by "extreme old age"—yet another variation on the theme of time. Lenina is horrified by a living example of the physical effects of temporal process. In the World State everyone remains young "almost unimpaired till sixty," when they then submit to state enforced euthanasia. Lenina's chronophobia is further reinforced by the snake dance, a fertility ceremony intended "to make the rain come and the corn grow" (137), that is, to celebrate the natural time of seasonal change and to draw together humanity and nature. The snake dance is the central event of the New Mexico trip, symbolizing—much in the manner of Bernard and Lenina's earlier trip over the English Channel—the raw and alien vigor of the natural world and humanity's connection to it. And to a degree this is the case. But Bernard and Lenina have crossed a threshold, not simply into an alien culture of natural instinct, emotions, and nonrational modes of perception, but a world that surprisingly mirrors the World State, albeit in strangely inverted ways.

While Malpais, with its costumes, rituals, music, and skin diseases, is a manifestly "queer" place, Lenina is forced to acknowledge that the snake dance was, at least initially, strikingly reminiscent of the communal Solidarity Services and Ford's Day celebrations of the World State. As the ritual gathers in intensity with the appearance of a troop of Indians costumed as monsters, who toss snakes about as they dance, Lenina becomes more and more upset. The ritual combines Indian and Christian elements, alternating between a fertility ceremony and a reenactment of Christ's suffering on the cross. The flagellation of the young boy marks the climax of the ritual, his blood presumably a reference to Christ's sacrifice and to the Indian god Pookong, who promises rain and fertility. The significance of this intensely sadistic ritual, however, lies less with the depiction of the snake dance itself than with its structural placement within Huxley's narrative. *Brave New World* began with an elaborate set piece, the detailed evocation of the Central London Hatchery. Bernard's tour of Malpais begins with the carefully detailed snake dance. Both are designed to exert human control over fertility and sexual reproduction. The Hatchery is a product of science; the snake dance is the result of a more primitive mode of perception. Both are attempts to bring the reproductive process, whether of human beings or of corn, under human control, but in utopia, God has been supplanted by technology. In Malpais, the Indian ritual is rooted in painful suffering, in nature, and in a relationship with natural processes that does not seem to involve their mastery or domination. In the Hatchery, nature is subjected to human reason in a world where natural processes have been harnessed to technological methods and goals.

These two extremes, the one excessively rationalized, the other irrational and primitively violent, meet in the Savage himself, the adopted son of an Indian and the natural son of a man and woman from the World State. John makes his appearance immediately following the fertility ritual. With pale blue eyes and a white skin, he is as much an outsider within his society as Bernard Marx is in his. Moreover, his first remarks are informed by the Elizabethan diction of Shakespeare. He identifies himself as "a most unhappy gentleman" and refers to the bloodstains from the fertility ritual as, in Lady Macbeth's words, a "damned spot," to which Lenina responds, "a gramme is better than a damn" (136). The rich language of *Hamlet* and *King Lear* is confronted by the bland commercial rhymes of the World State, yet it is the primitive who speaks the language of Shakespeare. John is closely linked to three important motifs: the family, sadomasochistic behavior, and language. He is a study in neurotic behavior, and his autobiography, a narrative about family and language, raises the central interpretive problem of *Brave New World*.

13

Sigmund Freud, Jean Jacques Rousseau, and John's Autobiography: Chapters 8–13

What is the reader to make of the Savage's thematic role in *Brave New World?* If Huxley is satirizing Wells's *Men Like Gods,* it would be reasonable to expect the bureaucratic technocracy of Mond's World State to be contrasted with a free, more unstructured realm of natural impulse. And to some extent this is the case. When John introduces himself to Bernard and Lenina his appearance immediately raises two of the dystopia's generic conventions noted in part 1. These are the oppositions of family and state, and nature and human culture. He instantly raises the basic distinction between civilization or "the Other Place" (136) and the pueblo of Malpais. He informs the visitors of his natural birth, and that he was abandoned by his father, whom he calls an "unnatural man" (138). But John, despite his childhood education among the Indians, is hardly a serenely natural man himself. His parents are both World State citizens, and from his earliest years he has been subject to World State values through the clumsy attempts of his mother, Linda, to educate him. Nevertheless, some critics have endeavored to view John as a version of Rousseau's natural man.

In his *Social Contract* (1762) and *The Discourse on the Origin of Inequality* (1755), the French philosopher Jean Jacques Rousseau theorized that humanity once existed in a prepolitical state of nature. Within such a hypothetical setting men and women were naturally good. Such a primitive individual or noble savage was corrupted by society, in particular, by the institutions of marriage and private property that were responsible for inequality, rivalry, and war. As noted earlier, Huxley believed that in "modern civilized societies the man, in Rousseau's words, is sacrificed to the citizen—the whole instinctive, emotional, physiological being is sacrificed to the specialized intellectual part of every man which permits" society to exist.[137] While he sympathized with such a conception of the natural individual repressed and distorted by modern social institutions and technology, he nevertheless rejected this concept as a utopian fiction. In *Proper Studies* he observed that "there are few people . . . who take the theories of Rousseau very seriously" and those who did were indulging in "a vague sentimental belief" in the virtues of some fictional "state of nature."[138]

The Savage, then, is not a study in Rousseau's noble savagery, not simply because the concept itself seemed to Huxley a sentimental delusion, but because John is hardly provided with the proper credentials. Both Malpais and the World State are dystopias, the latter a Wellsian nightmare, the former a primitivist fantasy. If Mustapha Mond's lecture on psychology, history, sexuality, and human development is the key interpretive text for the opening chapters of *Brave New World*, John's autobiography is the pivotal document for understanding the community of Malpais.

John's autobiographical narrative deliberately echoes the Director of Hatcheries' lecture on embryonic development and childhood training in the introductory chapters. The Director starts his lecture by saying "I shall begin at the beginning" (3). In chapter 8 Bernard instructs John to tell his story "from the beginning. As far back as you can remember" (145). John's story is a narrative of origins focusing on the development of self over a temporal span that again foregrounds the motifs of time and memory. His story is one of endless frustration, of the "crevice" or gap in time between desire and desire's satisfaction that Mustapha Mond fears as the source of personal emotion and thus of individual identity. In this context, it is a story about the acquisition of selfhood. It is also an emotionally charged narrative about personal and social rejection told to Bernard Marx, who himself feels rejected and marginalized. Finally, it is a story that would not be permitted in the World State because of its stress on ideologically prohibited subjects like motherhood and personal experience.

John's autobiography falls into twelve parts, beginning with the appearance of Popé, an adult male who locks him out of his mother's bedroom, and ending with John's exclusion from the Indian manhood ceremony, where he is pulled from the ranks of the other young men. In brief, it begins and ends with John's exclusion, first from the nuclear family and finally from the social community. In Mond's words, it is a record of the "suffocating intimacies" and "insane, obscene relationships between the members of the family group" (42). Worst of all, it is a personal history of what Mond hates, instability. John's personal experiences revolve around his mother, sexual shame, sadistic whippings, and the isolation of the perennial outsider. The disturbing effect of the intrusion of the male father figure, who separates him from his mother, is reinforced by his mother's promiscuity. Linda, a tourist accidentally abandoned in the Reservation, behaves in accordance with World State morality, but her sexual freedom is not acceptable in Malpais, where she is regarded as little better than a prostitute. The women of Malpais exclude her and finally punish her by whipping her. They also whip John, who is beaten by his mother as well. His story is a complex interweaving of shame and punishment centering on his confused response to his mother's promiscuity, a combination of sadistic punishment and masochistic guilt that will lead to his neurotic overidealization of women.

John's problems are compounded by Linda's attempts to educate him in the ways and values of World State civilization. She teaches him to read and then gives him her manual on embryo conditioning, an incomprehensible text that only increases his frustration. Ostracized by the other boys of Malpais, who sing insulting songs about his mother, John's only solace is a worn copy of *The Complete Works of William Shakespeare* discovered by Popé in an old chest.

Freud, Rousseau, and John's Autobiography

John's favorite play is *Hamlet*, which provides him with the language he needs to express his hatred of his rival for his mother's love. Indeed, Huxley suggests that his reading of Shakespeare's tragedy and his identification with the hero, Hamlet, leads directly to John's attack on Popé. This section of his story morbidly concentrates on the woman as prostitute and love as nothing more than gross sensuality. Hamlet's unrelenting preoccupation with corruption, incest, and prostitution is mirrored in John's obsession with his mother's behavior. The reader at this point might remember Bernard Marx's absorption with Lenina Crowne's "pneumatic" sexuality, especially his belief that she saw herself as just "so much meat" (63). John's increasing frustration, especially his twisted sense of women as unreliable, prone to sensuality and betrayal, is further consolidated by the loss of Kiakimé. The two ceremonies that conclude his autobiographical narrative are the climactic instances of all of John's anxieties and frustrations. In the first, the young Indian woman whom he loves, Kiakimé, is given to another man. In the second, John is prohibited from taking part in the manhood ritual because of his whiteness and his status as "the son of the she-dog." The result is complete isolation and despair: "He was all alone." Stoned by the other boys, he leaves the pueblo and wanders in the desert. Conscious only of his pain, he acts out the sufferings of "Jesus on the cross" and discovers "Time and Death and God" (162–63).

The Savage's story is hardly a celebration of an innocent primitive community in a paradisiacal state of nature. Malpais is Mustapha Mond's nightmare, a landscape run riot with all the impulses and forces that the World State, in order to exist, must repress and banish. To that extent it is a mirror image of Mond's controlled and sanitized technocracy. But in mirroring Mond's fears, Malpais does not automatically become a good or positive alternative to the World State. Mond repeatedly voices his opposition to individualism and personal identity. The World State exists to obliterate the temporal gap between desire and fulfillment. By making frustration and the emotions and feelings that accompany it impossible, Mond has removed the basis of self-awareness in suffering, temporal experience, and deferred desire.

In Malpais the Savage experiences nothing but pain and frustration, a process that leads to his discovery of time, death, and God. But his intensifying sense of personal identity that accompanies this enlargement of consciousness is crippled by a host of neurotic obsessions in relation to women, sexuality, punishment, and especially his mother. Early in *Brave New World* Mustapha Mond invokes Freud and instructs his students on "the appalling dangers of family life." The focal point for his attack on "family, monogamy, romance" is the mother, the symbol and actual cause "of every perversion from sadism to chastity" (44). John is shaped by Huxley in such a way as to make him the symbolic embodiment of Mustapha Mond's most irrational fears. John's thematic role, then, is not that of the virtuous, innocent, and prepolitical noble savage uncontaminated by the corruptions of social institutions. Rather, as the son of World State parents and partially educated in its values, he is also the partial product of those institutions and thus complicates Huxley's *Brave New World* in a number of conflicting ways. To fully grasp his role it is necessary to examine briefly his experiences in the World State, including his confrontation with Mustapha Mond himself.

Bernard returns to the World State accompanied by John and his mother. His plan is to bring back John and Linda as a scientific experiment, but his real motive is to expose and discredit the Director of Hatcheries, John's father. In a society permitting only laboratory pregnancies, to have naturally fathered a son is the ultimate disgrace. Bernard succeeds in his plot, and, as the patron of John, he becomes a social success as well, using the Savage as a means of attracting important guests to his parties and women to his bed. In chapters 9–11 Bernard is gradually displaced by the Savage as the novel's principal protagonist. In these chapters Bernard is revealed as an inherently shallow man whose chief goals are social acceptance and sexual pleasure. He cannot escape his behaviorist conditioning and, though he recognizes in John's autobiographical narrative a case of comparable loneliness and isolation, he cannot comprehend its larger significance.

As John takes over Bernard's role, he replaces him as the friend of Helmholtz Watson and the lover of Lenina Crowne. Bernard is still capable of criticizing World State culture, but his "carping unortho-doxy" (187) is relatively shallow when compared with John's increasingly horrified response to Mond's utopian society. John's tour of utopia occupies most of chapters 10–15. It is accompanied by the running commentary of Bernard's "scientific" report on John's reactions. His submersion in the systematically intensified sense experience of World State entertainment, like scent organ music and the feelies, only exacerbates his moral revulsion and culminates in his attempt to inspire a political rebellion at the Park Lane Hospital. Huxley, however, has carefully structured the book's conclusion around three pivotal encounters. In his autobiographical narrative, John tells of his wandering into the desert, where as a consequence of his spiritual and psychological despair, he discovered "Time and Death and God." His experiences in the World State will turn on these three interrelated subjects. Linda, his mother, will die. Mustapha Mond will discuss God and the soul with him, and his relationship with Lenina will involve a choice between the present time of immediate sensual satisfaction and more timeless values.

Before the climactic confrontation with Mustapha Mond, John is caught up, first, in his mother's death and then in Lenina's growing attraction to him. John, however, has difficulty separating the two women in his mind, obsessed as he is with a dualistic perception of women as saintly virgins and promiscuous whores. His inability to reconcile these conflicting responses lies at the heart of his sadomasochistic behavior in the novel's concluding chapters. In the case of Linda, she simply returns to the World State to die in a condition of drug-induced bliss. Her death is a form of hedonistic suicide. Drowning herself in *soma*, she loses her last "few years in time" as the drug ravages her body. Her "*soma*–holiday" is referred to as a form of "eternity" (184), but as she dies she returns to the temporal world, to the past and her memories of Popé. John, standing at the bedside, attempts to communicate with his dying mother, only to find himself confronted with Linda's memories of Popé. Furious with jealousy, he tries to "force her to come back from this dream of ignoble pleasures, from these base and hateful memories—back into the present, back into reality: the appalling present, the awful reality" (244). The single dominating fact of John's childhood was his mother's promiscuity and her being branded by the community of Malpais as a whore. The second major factor was John's rivalry with Popé for his mother's affections. Now, as Linda slowly dies, she does not recognize her son, and as John bends over and kisses her, she whispers "Popé," a word that strikes him in the face like "a pailful of ordure" (245). Horrified by the implications of this, he begins to shake her "because Popé was there in the bed" (245). She dies shortly after this scene and John believes that his violent actions were the cause of her death. Surrounded by a swarm of male twins brought to the hospital to be death-conditioned, John can only produce the one articulate word "God!" (248).

In Linda's death scene Huxley has brought to a climax two distinct themes that are at odds with each other and that complicate the resolution of *Brave New World*. First, the death itself, associated with *soma*, troops of genetically engineered twins, and Super-Wurlitzer music, is intended to emphasize the lengths to which the World State will go to mask or suppress the reality of fundamental human experiences. Huxley was fascinated by funerary practices, especially the desire to gloss over the reality of death by surrounding it with sentimental trappings. (His novel *After Many a Summer Dies the Swan* contains his most devastating attack on modern mortuary science.) Linda's death is robbed of all meaning by a society dedicated to the repression of all significant knowledge of time, temporal processes, birth, history, biography, and death itself. But Huxley has undermined the clear satirical thrust of the death scene. Instead of simply contrasting the mindless corruption of World State values with the dignity of John, who insists on mourning his mother and confronting death, Huxley transforms the death into a reenactment of sexual rivalry. Popé intervenes to yet again separate John from his mother. Instead of confronting death, John is faced with the old rival whom he once attempted to murder. In a frenzy of jealous rage and misery John attacks Linda and, after her death, takes responsibility for it. It is an ugly scene that reestablishes in the mind of the reader John's painful past and his neurotic obsession with his mother's promiscuity. In short, the World State's approach to the reality of death may be mindless and dishonest, but what has John to offer in its stead? He refuses the corrupt consolations of *soma* and conditioning, but his act of moral courage loses much of its force when the death scene becomes a reenactment of past emotional and sexual rivalry. John, it turns out, is as psychologically conditioned as Bernard Marx, not by means of behaviorist technique but as a result of repeated experiences of shame and rejection during his childhood. The focal point of such a prolonged education in humiliation and denial is Linda's role as mother and whore.

Huxley clarifies and accentuates this crucial aspect of John's past in the erotic episode with Lenina immediately prior to Linda's death scene. Lenina, going to John's apartment intending to seduce him, is not merely fended off but verbally assaulted by a man who sees women as simultaneously virginally pure and sensually corrupt. John idealizes Lenina, regarding her as a character out of Shakespeare's *Romeo and Juliet* or *The Tempest*. As a Juliet or a Miranda she exists as a happy, sentimental ideal of purity that vividly contrasts with the sordid reality of his mother. In John's eyes she is something to be "worthy of" (226), not ashamed of, and as such she functions as a compensatory ideal intended to redress the damage wrought by his mother. But when Lenina, not content to be worshipped, takes matters into her own hands and tries to seduce him, he draws back "in terror" as if she were "some intruding and dangerous animal." The scene that follows is both physically and mentally violent as John, overwhelmed by an "insane, inexplicable fury" (231), shouts epithets at her, especially the word "whore." Lenina has become Linda, the "impudent strumpet," and John reacts by pushing her to the ground and threatening to kill her. After driving her from the room, he repeats Lear's diatribe directed against the lust of women. Shakespeare's King Lear was mad and betrayed, so he thought, by all of his daughters. In drawing upon Lear's deranged attack on women as "Centaurs" (233), half-human and half-animal, Huxley has accentuated the Savage's neurotic obsession with prostitution and sensuality, a theme that pervades his autobiographical narrative and darkens his perception of Lenina, who now, for the first time, begins to look attractively normal. She is not, of course, and her vacuous sensuality is as unbalanced as John's neurotic asceticism.

In *Proper Studies* Huxley observed of the "powerful religion, or rather psuedo-religion, of sexual purity" that it tended to function as an inadequate and unhealthy substitute for more valid religious expression. He disliked puritanism and regarded extreme asceticism as morally dishonest and often as screening some form of repressed sexual desire. The puritan was, he argued, a fanatic: "Defined in psychological terms, a fanatic is a man who consciously overcompensates a secret doubt. The fanatics of puritanism are generally found to be overcompensating a secret prurience."[139] Huxley was fascinated by this character type; his most detailed exploration of the neurotic puritan occurs in *Point Counter Point* (Maurice Spandrell), his last novel prior to *Brave New World*. The Savage is such a fanatic, cherishing a distorted ideal of female purity that masks an obsession with sexual "prurience" and the woman as prostitute. His reading of Shakespeare's *Hamlet* and *King Lear* merely reinforces his revulsion for his mother's manifestly public eroticism. His heated brain, encumbered by the language of Hamlet and Lear, swings between the opposing extremes of fanatical idealism and vengeful violence. His preoccupation with what he takes to be his mother's betrayal and her uncontrollable sexuality morbidly insinuates itself into his attitude toward Lenina and, ultimately, toward everything he encounters in the World State. If Bernard Marx is denied a family, John appears to have had too much. If Bernard has no meaningful past, John is weighed down by the burden of his deeply troubled history. If Bernard's language is banal and simplistic, John's confused mingling of Shakespearean poetic diction and normal speech is grotesquely abstruse. Both characters are the perverted products of opposing extremes, the Wellsian futurist utopia and the "retrospective utopia" of the primitive past. Each, in fact, is a dystopia, a bad place, as the name Malpais suggests. John's criticism of Mond's World State and his attempt to spark a political revolution

Freud, Rousseau, and John's Autobiography

at the Park Lane Hospital are emotionally valid responses to Mond's technocracy, but they are primarily emotional—like so much of the Savage's behavior. It is not until chapters 16 and 17 that Huxley's novel attempts to clarify, if not resolve, the opposing sets of values dramatized in the characters of Mustapha Mond and the Savage.

14

Mustapha Mond
and the Defense of Utopia:
Chapters 14–18

In his portrait of Mustapha Mond, Huxley refused to summon the specter of totalitarianism, at least in its contemporary guise of a Mussolini or a Hitler. In his depiction of the World State he created a tyrannous and suffocating society governed not by Orwell's hard-faced dictator, but by the faceless bureaucrat dedicated to order and security. In Mond's world of compliant slaves there is no need for the ruthlessness of a Stalin. The fundamental political axiom of Mond's utopia is the belief that to achieve stability one must first stabilize the workers. The goal of the council of Ten World Controllers is absolute political stability, which requires a society of useful, obedient citizens. The technocratic Controllers have created a vast impersonal system in which people are designed to match the commodities they produce. Mond does not need to reach the minds of his citizens; he can simply create them.

Bernard Marx's fellow workers are conditioned to political subjection in a society so completely commercialized that all of its values are grounded in the economic requirements of state capitalism. Within such a paradisiacal socialist collective, everybody belongs to everybody else "in the interests of industry" (58). Both socialist and capitalist, the World State is the Weberian bureacrat's dream of acquiescent, perfectly manipulable workers and technicians in a stable, vertical hierarchy (Alpha to Epsilon). Mustapha Mond's role of Controller corresponds to that of a super factory manager in a Taylorized world of docile workers. Such unthinking consent to authority rules out the possibility of political opposition, and thus Mond feels no need for public demonstration of the punitive power of the state.

Mond, however, is a more complex figure than his role as World Controller suggests. In chapter 16, Bernard Marx, Helmholtz Watson, and John, the Savage, are taken to the Controller's study. Their abortive revolution at the Park Lane Hospital has foundered on the inability of genetically engineered and psychologically conditioned workers to even comprehend the notion of political opposition. The confrontation between the presumably natural and free Savage and the order-loving bureaucrat begins immediately after the reference to Henry Ford's autobiography, lying on a study table. As noted in chapter 4 of this volume, Ford's autobiography is the sacred text of the World State, just as the Savage's autobiographical narration in chapter 8 is the chief document about Malpais and its culture. John and Mond, however, meet on the one ground they share in common, the plays of Shakespeare, trading quotations from *The Tempest* and arguing about the value of art. Mond's first significant statement is an assertion of raw power, one of the few (arguably the only) gestures he makes in the direction of crude dictatorial authority. After admitting that he has read Shakespeare, he says that such an activity is prohibited to most of the population, adding, "but as I make the laws here, I can also break them" (262). Mond is openly asserting his membership in an intellectual elite. As "one of the very few" (262), he functions as part of an oligarchy, a minority endowed with something approaching absolute power but also conditioned and engineered genetically for its position. The Controllers can make and break the law, but the extent of their freedom is still limited; they control society but they too are its product. The final source of power in the World State is the World State itself, a vast and, in Mond's words, "irresistible machine" (266) that encloses and sustains everyone.

As the spokesman of such a self-perpetuating organization, Mond defines its essence as a kind of industrial prison dedicated to the achievement of perpetual "stability," his favorite word. Indeed, he boasts that the Controllers have created "the stablest equilibrium in history" (272) and defines society as a collective patient that requires the ministrations of a bureaucracy that acts as a medical-industrial staff. In one of his most significant statements, Mond tells the Savage that the World State is the final product of an "industrial civilization" that places no restrictions on the material appetites of its workers. To ensure social and commercial equilibrium it systematically fosters "self-indulgence up to the very limits imposed by hygiene and economics" (284). Those last two nouns encapsulate the goals of the Controllers and define their function as bureaucratic technicians. Mond sees himself as a doctor who inoculates his patient with drugs. Such a narcotized population requires the "infantile and embryonic fixations" (287) of *soma* and the material security of guaranteed commodity markets. The World State worker is both patient and "goods-consuming citizen" (283), as well as a technically designed component in a vast social mechanism.

As the Savage listens to Mond's exposition of World State economy, he periodically raises objections that are quickly dismissed by the Controller. Many of John's attempts to resist the logical force of Mond's arguments are vaguely aesthetic, weak attempts to register his emotional revulsion for the vulgar commercialization of World State culture. Knowing little about scientific methodology, he is unequipped to oppose Mond's surprising rejection of science. In chapter 12 Huxley creates a brief scene in which Mond reads and assesses "A New Theory of Biology," admiring the ingenuity of its arguments but refusing to allow its publication. Mond's objections focus on the author's belief in historical progress, on a historical goal that has not been realized in the World State but instead "was somewhere beyond, somewhere outside the present human sphere." Such an explanation "in terms of purpose" proposes a future mental advance on the part of collective humanity consisting of "some intensification and refining of consciousness, some enlargement of knowledge" (211). For Mond,

Mustapha Mond and the Defense of Utopia

this speculative theory is "potentially subversive" because it raises again—only in more sweeping terms—the one thing Mond fears the most, the gap or crevice in time between desire and fulfillment. Mond's fear of time and deferred happiness is as neurotic as the Savage's preoccupation with chastity and sexual purity. Mond worships stability, which can only be achieved and maintained by a coercive emphasis on "the present human sphere" where "the purpose of life was . . . the maintenance of well-being" (211). The quintessential bureaucrat, he cherishes order and control within an unchanging routine: "We don't want to change. Every change is a menace to stability. . . . Every discovery in pure science is potentially subversive; even science must sometimes be treated as a possible enemy. Yes, even science" (269). Whatever goals exist for humanity, they must be satisfied here, now, in the eternal present of the World State.

In chapter 17 Mond confronts what Huxley regards as the ultimate challenge to the technocratic utopia of the Controllers—religion. Bertrand Russell, in *The Scientific Outlook*, also speculated about the appearance of a scientific global state governed by technocratic bureaucrats like Mustapha Mond. But Huxley's emphasis on religion, and especially on Mond's sympathy with religious thinkers like William James and Maine de Biran, introduces a more complex note. Mond's study safe contains a secret cache of theoretical books, including Thomas à Kempis's *The Imitation of Christ*, William James's *The Varieties of Religious Experience,* and the Bible. It is worth noting that the safe does not contain "heretical" works of pure science like those of Newton or Einstein. In Mond's view, the most dangerously destabilizing books are those of theologians or philosophers like Cardinal Newman or Maine de Biran. This emphasis on religious experience at the conclusion of *Brave New World* is another feature of Huxley's dystopia that differentiates it from the futurist narratives of Wells and Zamiatin. If Huxley and Zamiatin had turned the tables on Wells by reversing the binary oppositions of science and nature and attacking Wells's idealization of science, Huxley has taken the further steps of, first, undermining the status of nature and the primitivist utopia as an alternative to the Wellsian scientific utopia, and, second, introducing

God and religion as a tentatively conceived solution to what he regarded as the unworkable and sterile opposition of science and nature.
If Mond's technocratic World State is a debased utopia pandering to
self-indulgent materialism and recognizing only the restraints of "hygiene and economics," the predictable alternative ought to be a more
humane community, a sphere of freedom and instinctual experience
more closely allied to natural processes and rhythms. But Huxley, in
discrediting both the Wellsian scientific utopia and the primitivist "retrospective utopia," turns to the possibility of an order of experience
beyond history, science, and nature.

In chapter 17 Mustapha Mond reads to John a series of lengthy
passages from his favorite theologians and philosophers. He chooses
those sections that offer a rationale for *both* religion and the World
State. The essence of his argument is directed against the Savage's "old
romantic" liberalism, his belief in freedom and the autonomous self.
What Mond is most eager to discredit is John's faith in temporal
experience, in the progressive intensification and refinement of individual consciousness. Love, poetry, and Shakespeare are not, in the Savage's view, incompatible with a belief in God. Mond, however, fears
anything that cannot be controlled and directed toward his supreme
goal of the unchanging stability of a timeless present. Accordingly, his
examples from theology stress two basic conclusions: humanity is not
fit for independence of any kind, and, in a dangerous and potentially
chaotic world, the means must be found so that humanity can be
carried "safely to the end" (279).

The quotations from Maine de Biran, a late eighteenth-century
French philosopher, and Cardinal Newman, a nineteenth-century British theologian, are carefully selected to coincide with Mond's own
prejudices. The passage from Newman declares that "we cannot be
supreme over ourselves. We are not our own masters" (278). Newman
is arguing that individuals belong to God, but the quotation aligns
itself nicely with World State ideology. The citizens of Mond's utopia
are clearly not their own masters. They have no selves to speak of, and
belong, not to God, but to the collective community. Thus, Newman's
religious judgment that "independence was not made for man" (279)

is indistinguishable from the fundamental political assumptions of the World State itself.

The second passage (from de Biran) is an expression of Mond's deepest anxiety, the fear of old age, temporal change, and death. De Biran writes of the "sickness of old age" and turning to God as the individual becomes less capable of enjoying the life of the senses and less distracted by passion and physical desires, "whereupon God emerges as from behind a cloud" (279). Mond retorts that "the modern world" promises "youth and prosperity right up to the end," and, as a result, "there aren't any losses for us to compensate; religious sentiment is superfluous" (280). Despite this, Mond believes that a god probably exists, but after the establishment of the World State, he only "manifests himself as an absence; as though he weren't there at all" (281). Mond's technocracy has displaced God and history. Its appearance has relegated concepts of eternity to a kind of limbo; they are simply not relevant. It has done away with ideas of past and future. History is irrelevant, and no future goals exist to be attained. This obliteration of past, future, and eternity leaves only one category of time—the present. This Mond defends with gusto: "God isn't compatible with machinery and scientific medicine and universal happiness" (281). Neither is history, because historical time implies change and Mond's machinery has been perfected by what he calls "the people who organize society" (283), the elite of bureaucratic technicians. As for the inhabitant of this utopia, Mond flatly pronounces him beyond improvement: "As a happy, hard-working, goods-consuming citizen he's perfect" (283).

The Savage saves what he thinks is his strongest card until the end, raising his principal ethical objection in such a way that it complicates both the debate and the resolution of Huxley's novel. After Mond has read and commented on the passages from Newman and de Biran and pronounced the World State perfect, John asks, "What about self-denial, then?" (284). If Mond is neurotically obsessed with time and change, John is fanatically self-renunciatory. Mond, who fears time, especially loathes the female, whom he links to the temporal process of birth and death. His language on the subject of female

sexuality, and especially childbirth, is intemperate, even faintly pathological. Similarly, John is mired in morbid thoughts about female promiscuity, especially as it touches upon Lenina's and his mother's lives.
The Mond who rants in chapter 3 about "obscene relationships" and
"the darkness, disease, and smells" of family life is not much different
from the Savage who screams "whore! Impudent strumpet!" at Lenina
and evokes female sexuality in terms of "darkness . . . burning, scald-
ing, stench, consumption" (233). Mond almost always focuses his
streams of verbal abuse at the image of the mother, and John's violent
language is traceable to his family experiences and his mother's dominant role within them.

Self-denial, then, for John, has a particular meaning. Though he
feels a general revulsion for the hedonism and commercialized pleasures of World State society, he reserves his most virulent scorn for
Lenina's sexual candor and openness. A romantic idealist whose exaggerated ideal of female purity functions to compensate for his mother's
erotic behavior in Malpais, he focuses on chastity as the ultimate form
of self-denial. Mond sweeps such an objection aside, linking chastity
with irrational passion and "neurasthenia" (284). To the extent that
John is clearly neurotic, Mond is correct. As a young man who has
been raised by a mother ill prepared for the responsibilities of parent-
hood, who was a witness to his mother's public beating and her sexual
activities, who was himself humiliated by his mother's lover and rejected by his social peers, and who, finally, has received a thoroughly
contradictory education, half garbled fragments about the World State
and half tribal myth, the Savage is a study in neurotic instability. And
as such, he is living proof of Mond's contention that the Savage's
espousal of chastity merely screens a secret fixation on female sexuality. In short, he is emotionally disturbed and, thus, socially unstable.

John persists in his efforts to refute the easy flow of Mond's
words, seemingly logical and comforting in their defense of order and
soma-induced happiness. Unable to provoke a genuinely human response from this oligarchic bureaucrat, he finally objects that "nothing
costs enough here" (287). The World State, founded on the carefully
regulated production of consumer commodities, is dedicated to keep-

ing the costs down in every way possible. Accordingly, John's metaphor of price is aptly chosen. Mond's utopia comes, ironically, at too high a price in human dignity, freedom, and individuality, and so, John, liberal to the end, claims what Mond can only see as "the right to be unhappy" (288). The problem, of course, is that John is a self-destructive neurotic, and his choice of unhappiness, that is, his preference for self-discipline and self-development over a period of time in which goals are distant and not crudely materialist, is dramatized by Huxley as motivated by his distorted emotions. In short, John's moral ideas are simply neurotic symptoms.

If Mond is obsessed with the "eternal present," John is crippled by the traumatic past. Mond is fearful of the future and buries his head in the sensual gratifications of the present. John, scarred by the past of his childhood, projects his pain into a future of unattainable ideals. The root of this dilemma lies, at least in part, with the status of women in *Brave New World*, both as sex objects and chaste ideals. It manifests itself most vividly in the novel's climactic final chapter, a scene of sadomasochistic violence and suicidal despair. In choosing the right to unhappiness, John has chosen isolation and independence. He retreats from the distractions and frivolities of the World State and occupies a deserted lighthouse where he plans to live a life of monkish asceticism. The religious motifs of the concluding chapter (references to Christ's crucifixion, purification, prayer, flagellation, hermitage) reinforce the ostensibly spiritual nature of John's decision to reject the things of Mond's world. But John is also rejecting Lenina, and it is her reappearance that finally destroys him. Of his two adversaries, Mond is the easier if not to overcome, at least to defy. Huxley has characterized Mond as a man who, even when he speculates on a society of Alphas as an alternative to his own utopian society, can only conceive of them as conditioned for "making a free choice and assuming responsibilities" (266). He cannot imagine an unconditioned world. Mond is also emotionally unbalanced in his fixation on the loathsome nature of motherhood and oddly secretive, as his collection of secret books shows. He is capable of boasting of his power to break laws, and in his reference to "the lethal chamber" (274) the faceless bureaucrat gives way, momentarily, to the hard-faced dictator. John can ultimately repudiate Mond's ideology, but Lenina's attraction is more fundamental and troubling.

At the lighthouse, John begins by renouncing the materialist and technological values of the World State, but as the chapter proceeds, he focuses more and more intently on the disciplining of erotic desire. He attempts to establish his own utopia of one, a state of isolated individualism contrasted with the tribal culture of Malpais and the collectivist technocracy of the World State. He chooses manual labor, purchasing only hand tools in his endeavor to revert back to the "retrospective utopia" of nature, instinct, and primitivist values. His real motivation, however, is not the broadly liberal emphasis of his conversation with Mond. There he defended art, political liberty, and pure science (a term he barely understood). At the lighthouse, however, John's behavior is inspired by his sense of guilt, personal depravity, and some unspecified form of contamination. It takes the form of sadomasochistic self-punishment and culminates in suicide by way of a sexual orgy.

Early in *Brave New World,* Mustapha Mond had said that a world "full of mothers" was a world full "therefore of every kind of perversion from sadism to chastity" (44). This link between sadistic violence and erotic self-discipline is the principal focus of Huxley's concluding chapter, a scene of nihilistic mayhem reminiscent of the writings of the Marquis de Sade. The question for the reader is, why did Huxley choose this way of bringing his narrative to closure? How does it resolve the conventional problem of the modern utopia or dystopia—the opposition between science and nature or reason and emotion? In *Proper Studies* Huxley theorized about the relationship between the conscious and unconscious mind, and the human tendency to pursue extremes: "Suppressed in the conscious mind, which is occupied exclusively with its noble and disinterested cause, the personal, self-regarding tendencies 'get their own back' in the unconscious. The unconscious state of mind is in contradiction with the conscious." He then added: "Thus we frequently observe that the consciously convinced puritan is deeply preoccupied in his uncon-

134

scious mind with precisely those sexual matters which he professes to hate."[140] This is a succinct diagnosis of the Savage's predicament, and explains the tortured emotions that govern his actions in the concluding chapter. What haunts John is not Mond and his arguments but the conscious memory of his dead mother and his unconscious memory of her status as prostitute in Malpais. All of this accumulated guilt is compensated for by means of a self-punishing idealization of woman as angelically pure and nonsexual. The challenge to this is the very physical Lenina Crowne and John's all-too-evident desire for her—which he is determined to suppress.

John has been violent with both women, slapping Lenina when she attempted to seduce him and shaking his mother as she lay on her deathbed. At the lighthouse he begins what is a program of religious self-discipline with acts of physical self-mortification. He tortures his body by assuming poses of "voluntary crucifixion," extending his arms for long periods of time in order to induce "excruciating agony" (292), and prays "to be good" despite the fact that he has done nothing wrong. The key to this cycle of increasingly self-destructive behavior occurs when, after breaking into song because of his enjoyment of his work, he whips himself bloody with a knotted cord. John has been associated with whips from the beginning of Huxley's narrative. He had hoped to be beaten during the snake dance, at the very point of his introduction in the narrative. Lenina incredulously asked, "Do you mean to say that you *wanted* to be hit with that whip?" (137). Later, John was witness to his mother's whipping by the other women of Malpais, and was whipped in turn by them, as well as beaten by his mother. The flagellation scenes at the lighthouse are a further development of this pattern of transgression, punishment, and purification. John is driven by his pervasive sense of guilt; rejected by his mother and by his community, humiliated by her sexual promiscuity and by his own desire for Lenina, John can only see women in terms of fanatically extreme oppositions. His childhood experiences have given rise to a complex schizophrenic image of women as either saints or prostitutes, chaste virgins or sensually appetitive whores. His self-punishing asceticism masks a "secret prurience," and Lenina's arrival at the lighthouse triggers John's mental breakdown as well as a sexual orgy.

The climactic scene of mayhem that brings Huxley's narrative to its bleak conclusion is an exercise in the grotesque. Surrounded by Mond's mindless utopians, who demand "the whipping stunt" (307), and paralyzed by the arrival of Lenina, John surrenders to all of his demons. Earlier, suddenly thinking of Lenina's body, he has whipped himself to drive away the seductive image, shouting "strumpet" at every blow as though his own bleeding body was hers: "And how frantically, without knowing it, he wished it were" (302). Huxley's interjection emphasizes the role of unconscious mental behavior in all of John's actions. When Lenina actually arrives in the final scene at the lighthouse, John's ferocity is a direct expression of his desire for her. Violence, and especially sadomasochistic whipping, is the only channel left for the expression of his guilt-twisted love. The crowd of World State onlookers, in a childishly blurred way, recognize this and, as he alternately whips Lenina and himself, begin to beat each other, forming a circle and dancing to the refrain of "Orgy-porgy." Significantly, the Savage awakens the next day from what Huxley calls "a long-drawn frenzy of sensuality" (310), not spiritual self-discipline. John, then, is Huxley's puritan who is "deeply preoccupied in his unconscious mind with precisely those sexual matters which he professes to hate." In this respect, the orgy is a fitting symbol for narrative closure. It exemplifies the mindless materialism of Mond's World State that, in its erotic aspect, lies hidden even within the psyche of the World State's principal antagonist. Accordingly, John's suicide is a final act of self-punishment that mirrors his earliest appearance in the text, where he wished to be ritually punished. Equally important, his suicidal impulse is activated by an act of memory. He awoke and "then suddenly remembered—everything." Memory, as I emphasized earlier, is forbidden in the World State, where personal memories are seen as contributing to individualism and the past is regarded as irrelevant to the utopian present. John, individualist to the end, is, ironically, destroyed by the very faculty that promotes and sustains personal identity. Again, Mond appears to be vindicated.

Mustapha Mond and the Defense of Utopia

The final question posed by chapter 18 is how to integrate it with
the overarching theme of *Brave New World*, the dystopian nature of the
technocratic World State. There are several possible answers to this
question; three are particularly persuasive and interesting. The out-
standing feature of Huxley's conclusion is that everyone is discredited
to some degree. Mond, who apparently wins his argument with the
Savage and continues to rule the World State, which presumably continues to flourish as a technocratic utopia, is gradually revealed to be the
quintessential Weberian bureaucrat. He cannot really comprehend
John's half-formed liberalism, and he appears to be as perverted as John
when he turns to the subject of the maternal female. The Savage, as we
have just seen, is thoroughly neurotic in his puritanical fanaticism and
sadomasochistic behavior. Contrasted with the rather lurid energies of
the Savage, Bernard Marx is simply dismissed in the latter half of the
narrative. After the Malpais chapters he is treated as a shallow, insecure,
and improperly conditioned Alpha, who is conveniently banished to
Iceland. Finally, Lenina has no role to speak of; she exists only as an
object of desire to be either pursued or avoided. The single interesting
feature that Huxley permits her is her apparent need for a sustained
relationship with one man rather than the socially sanctioned promiscuity of the World State. Huxley's conclusion, then, with its emphasis on
violence, infantile sensuality, and suicide, is a thoroughly bleak rendering of a world that offers no escape from the deformative influences of
World State technology. The question is why Huxley was impelled to
write such an aridly pessimistic conclusion.

In *Men Like Gods*, Wells's scientific reformers succeed in subduing
the ancestral man-ape and creating a rational democratic utopia. In
Zamiatin's *We*, the somewhat apelike revolutionaries from behind the
Green Wall attempt to restore the balance by attacking the scientific
tyranny of the glass city, a rebellion still continuing at the narrative's
conclusion. In *Brave New World*, the Wellsian scientific utopia is conceived as an oppressive dystopia, yet no possibility of a restoration of
instinctual or natural values is permitted. There are three distinct yet
related explanations for this. The first turns on Huxley's philosophy of
history during the interwar period. The cultural trauma of the First

World War, reinforced by the rise of what Huxley referred to as new romanticism with its emphasis on collectivist politics and mechanization and its scorn for liberalism, had engendered a society that Huxley, like many of his contemporaries, viewed as self-destructive or suicidal. Accordingly, the "insane ideals" of Europe and America in the late twenties and early thirties are reflected—in grotesquely magnified ways—in the neurotic behavior of Mond and the Savage. Huxley's analysis of European history and its suicidal tendencies have been discussed in part one. At this stage it is sufficient to note the close connection between Huxley's use of sadomasochistic motifs in his discussions of contemporary history and the centrality of sadomasochistic acts in *Brave New World*. The climactic scene at the lighthouse dramatizes the sheer meaninglessness of the Marquis de Sade's self-indulgent materialism. John, of course, is the victim of a series of deformative childhood experiences that have rendered him incapable of a balanced and normal response to women. In this respect, he cannot be reduced to an example of an aggressive and power-hungry nihilist like the Earl of Gonister in *After Many a Summer Dies the Swan* or Coleman of *Antic Hay*. Nevertheless, it can be argued that the entire scene at the lighthouse, its violence and nihilistic despair culminating in the excesses of an orgy and a suicide, exemplifies the philosophy of meaninglessness that Huxley associated with the word "sadomasochistic." The final scene, then, registers Huxley's own despair over the increasingly irrational course of modern history.

Such an interpretation also explains another puzzling feature of Huxley's dystopia. The nihilistic materialism of the World State, including its worship of comfort and pleasure, cannot be escaped. As a manifestation of a cultural trend that Huxley perceived in modern Europe and America, it dominates his narrative to the extent that no real alternative is permitted. Huxley refused to juxtapose the technocratic World State with a wholly natural setting like the wild forests of Zamiatin's Green World. For Huxley, such a choice between technological civilization and a natural sphere of instinctual spontaneity was a delusion; it simply was no longer relevant. The Savage is not really a savage, but a product of both the World State and Malpais. Both are dystopias and both equally pernicious in their effects on John. Huxley believed that the social and economic trends permeating modern culture could not be addressed by means of an appeal to simplified categories like nature and noble savagery. New romantic ideas had insinuated themselves into all aspects of human experience and had to be portrayed for what they were, universally pervasive ideologies that threatened the very essence of what it meant to be human.

A second approach to the meaning of chapters 17 and 18 turns on the theme of religion. From the Savage's first appearance in the narrative, he is closely linked to religious experiences of various kinds. The final confrontation with Mustapha Mond culminates in an exchange on God and religion, and the Savage's retreat to the lighthouse is conceived in religious terms. The first interpretation construes the closing chapters as composing a vision of nihilism, of sadomasochistic anarchy in a world in which meaning and hope are completely absent. Mond, however, defines God as an absence whose reappearance presumably would restore meaning to the world. If the key to Huxley's vision of a dystopian society is the absence of God, then this would offer a different way of explaining the absence of a consistently natural realm in opposition to Mond's technocratic utopia. The true alternative to the World State is not the primitivist's innocent nature but a spiritual truth transcending both science and nature.

Mond's utopia is a secular culture where religion has been replaced by the worship of Our Ford and Our Freud. Malpais preserves some kind of religious experience, only muddled and sadistically violent. Jesus and Pookong have been run together in an eclectic religion stressing seasonal cycles and fertility. The difficulty with this assessment of Huxley's conclusion is that John's spiritual cravings flow from his sadomasochistic neurosis. He prizes chastity because of his revulsion for his mother's promiscuity, and he whips himself in order to punish himself as a consequence of his desires for Lenina. Huxley, it would appear, has discredited the religious theme from the very outset by linking John's quest for spiritual truth with his perverted puritanism and psychological aberrations. It can be argued, however, that both John and Mond see through a glass darkly, Mond worshipping stability and technology, and the Savage unable to escape his past. The truth contained, for example, in the theological passages of chapter 17 remains just that, the truth, but out of reach of the complacent technocrat and the neurotic Savage. The final episode of chapter 18, then, can be viewed as a harrowing depiction of a world without transcendent or spiritual meaning. Such a reading, moreover, conforms to the muted religious theme in Huxley's work of the twenties, where a number of his novels, particularly *Those Barren Leaves* and *Point Counter Point,* raise the issue of some barely intuited level of spiritual being. The chief objection to such a reading, however, lies in the sheer futility of John's beliefs, especially their neurotic origins. In *Brave New World,* religion is introduced primarily as an illusory projection of twisted desires traceable to John's childhood traumas.

The third approach to the meaning of the final scene can be traced to Lenina's pivotal question, "What's time for?" (104). Mond's answer would be the achievement of the World State through carefully controlled technological progress. Time, for Mond, is, like nature, something to be mastered, to be safely confined to the eternal present of his utopian technocracy. Once the World State is established even history and progress are pretty much irrelevant. For John, time is the medium in which the individual self grows and develops. At Malpais, time is the cycle of seasons, of planting and harvesting in accordance with nature's temporal rhythms. As the author of his own autobiographical narrative, John has a self and a memory that are interdependent; self is constituted out of the recollected past. Perhaps, too, the soul can only advance toward the eternity of godhead through the medium of time. Lenina, however, is never given an answer. Mond, in his quest for social stability, has deprived her of her natural role of mother. John, neurotically fixated on exaggerated notions of feminine purity, has denied her her sexuality. The passages he quotes from Shakespeare alternately praise virginal ideals or condemn promiscuous sensualists. The last significant event in the narrative prior to John's suicide is the beating of a woman. In chapter 3 Bernard Marx complains that Lenina "thinks of herself as meat" (62), a surprising insight. Indeed, Bernard's observation is the only potentially liberating

Mustapha Mond and the Defense of Utopia

perception of women in all of *Brave New World*. He knows that
Lenina has been reduced to an object and that such degradation includes himself as well. But Huxley never permits Bernard's revolutionary insight to develop and flourish; he shifts the focus to the perverted
Savage and his self-destructive guilt. Between Mond's hysterical antipathy for maternity and John's neurotic fear of female sexuality, women
have no significant role in Huxley's dystopia—a deliberate omission
that gives his novel its peculiar atmosphere of incompleteness or, perhaps more accurately, its genuinely dystopic theme. Time, history,
seasonal cycles, memory, and human development have all been arrested in Mond's static world, and fundamental to the maintenance of
such controlled sterility is the obliteration of female sexuality in its
relation to the reproductive cycle itself. In such a world of patriarchal
technology the predominantly male ruling caste has achieved its dream
of absolute mastery.

Notes

1. Aldous Huxley, *Letters of Aldous Huxley,* ed. Grover Smith (London: Chatto & Windus, 1969), 383–84.

2. Huxley, *Letters,* 224.

3. Aldous Huxley, *Point Counter Point* (1928; London: Chatto & Windus, 1963), 408.

4. Aldous Huxley, *Ends and Means* (New York: Harper & Brothers, 1937), 24.

5. Huxley, *Point Counter Point,* 161.

6. Huxley, *Letters,* 356.

7. Theodor W. Adorno, *Negative Dialectics,* trans. E. B. Ashton (New York: Continuum, 1987), 320.

8. Huxley, *Letters,* 391.

9. Christopher Lasch, *The Minimal Self: Psychic Survival in Troubled Times* (New York: W. W. Norton, 1984), 47.

10. *Aldous Huxley: The Critical Heritage,* ed. Donald Watt (London: Routledge & Kegan Paul, 1975), 204.

11. Quoted in Sybille Bedford, *Aldous Huxley: A Biography* (New York: Alfred A. Knopf/Harper & Row, 1974), 253.

12. Quoted by Watt, "Introduction," *Critical Heritage,* 16.

13. Watt, *Critical Heritage,* 198, 202.

14. Watt, *Critical Heritage,* 204.

15. J. B. S. Haldane, "Biological Possibilities for the Human Species in the Next Ten Thousand Years" in *Man and His Future,* ed. Gordon Wolstenholme (London: J. & A. Churchill, 1963), 340; Gordon Rattray Taylor, *The Biological Time-Bomb* (London: Thames & Hudson, 1968), 43.

16. Watt, *Critical Heritage,* 214.

17. Watt, *Critical Heritage,* 209.

18. Watt, *Critical Heritage,* 333–34.

19. Judith N. Shklar, *After Utopia: The Decline of Political Faith* (Princeton: Princeton University Press, 1957), 155.

20. Peter Edgerly Firchow, *The End of Utopia: A Study of Aldous Huxley's "Brave New World"* (Lewisburg: Bucknell University Press, 1984), 79.

21. Watt, *Critical Heritage*, 212.

22. Watt, *Critical Heritage*, 333.

23. Laurence Brander, *Aldous Huxley: A Critical Study* (Lewisburg: Bucknell University Press, 1970), 65.

24. Bernard Crick, "Critical Introduction" to George Orwell, *Nineteen Eighty-Four* (1949; Oxford: Clarendon Press, 1984), 9.

25. Watt, *Critical Heritage*, 17, 346.

26. Watt, *Critical Heritage*, 214.

27. Watt, *Critical Heritage*, 221–22.

28. Watt, *Critical Heritage*, 224, 226.

29. Watt, *Critical Heritage*, 227.

30. Watt, *Critical Heritage*, 172.

31. Watt, *Critical Heritage*, 175.

32. Jerome Meckier, *Aldous Huxley: Satire and Structure* (London: Chatto & Windus, 1969), 37, 39.

33. Philip Thody, *Aldous Huxley: A Biographical Introduction* (New York: Charles Scribner's Sons, 1973), 52.

34. Watt, *Critical Heritage*, 446.

35. George Woodcock, *Dawn and the Darkest Hour: A Study of Aldous Huxley* (London: Faber and Faber, 1972), 87, 14.

36. George Orwell, *Nineteen Eighty-Four*, ed. Bernard Crick (1949; Oxford: Clarendon Press, 1984), 319–20.

37. Watt, *Critical Heritage*, 202.

38. Watt, *Critical Heritage*, 202.

39. Huxley, *Letters*, 604.

40. Huxley, *Letters*, 605.

41. Aldous Huxley, *Proper Studies* (1927; London: Chatto & Windus, 1957), 137.

42. Huxley, *Letters*, 348.

43. Quoted in Christopher Collins, *Evgenij Zamjatin: An Interpretive Study* (The Hague: Mouton, 1973), 41.

44. Aldous Huxley, *The Olive Tree* (London: Chatto & Windus, 1936), 135.

45. Huxley, *The Olive Tree*, 135.

Notes

46. H. G. Wells, *Men Like Gods*, vol. 28 of *The Works of H. G. Wells* (New York: Charles Scribner's Sons, 1927), 107–8.

47. Wells, *Men Like Gods*, 263, 278.

48. Wells, *Men Like Gods*, 266.

49. Wells, *Men Like Gods*, 77, 71.

50. Wells, *Men Like Gods*, 72.

51. Wells, *Men Like Gods*, 72.

52. Wells, *Men Like Gods*, 76–77.

53. Wells, *Men Like Gods*, 78.

54. Wells, *Men Like Gods*, 80.

55. Wells, *Men Like Gods*, 313–14.

56. H. G. Wells, *The Sleeper Awakes*, vol. 2 of *The Works of H. G. Wells* (New York: Charles Scribner's Sons, 1924), 392.

57. A brief discussion of this issue can be found in Christopher Collins's *Evgenij Zamjatin: An Interpretive Study*. See page 41 (especially footnote 1). Alex M. Shane offers a more detailed analysis on page 140 of *The Life and Works of Evgenij Zamjatin*. (Berkeley: University of California Press, 1968). There is little agreement on the spelling of Zamiatin's name in English.

58. Yevgeny Zamyatin, *We*, trans. Mirra Ginsburg (New York: Avon, 1983), 5.

59. Zamiatin, *We*, 61, 214.

60. Huxley, *Olive Tree*, 135.

61. Huxley, *Olive Tree*, 134.

62. A. L. Rowse, *Science and History: A New View of History* (New York: W. W. Norton, 1928), 13.

63. John Strachey, *The Coming Struggle for Power* (New York: Covici, Friede, 1933), 274.

64. John Maynard Keynes, *Essays in Biography* (New York: Harcourt, Brace, 1933), 91.

65. Stephen Spender, *The Destructive Element: A Study of Modern Writers and Beliefs* (London: Jonathan Cape, 1935), 223.

66. Aldous Huxley, "The Outlook for American Culture," *Harper's Magazine*, August 1927, 270.

67. Huxley, "Outlook for American Culture," 270.

68. H. A. L. Fisher, *Pages from the Past* (Oxford: Clarendon Press, 1939), p. vi.

69. H. A. L. Fisher, Foreword, *The Liberal Experiment*, vol. 3 of *A History of Europe* (Boston: Houghton Mifflin, 1936).

70. Fisher, *Liberal Experiment*, 1254–56.

71. Fisher, *Liberal Experiment*, 1195.

72. Huxley, *Proper Studies*, xv.

73. Aldous Huxley, *Do What You Will* (London: Chatto & Windus, 1929), 29.

74. Huxley, *Do What You Will*, 295.

75. Huxley, *Olive Tree*, 23.

76. Huxley, *Olive Tree*, 23.

77. Aldous Huxley, *Music at Night* (1931; London: Chatto & Windus, 1960), 212.

78. Huxley, *Music at Night*, 213–14.

79. Huxley, *Music at Night*, 212, 215, 219.

80. Huxley, *Music at Night*, 220.

81. Huxley, *Ends and Means*, 24.

82. Huxley, *Proper Studies*, 9.

83. See, for example, David McLellan's *Ideology* (Minneapolis: University of Minnesota Press, 1986), especially pages 82 and 83.

84. Huxley, *Proper Studies*, 270.

85. Stephen Spender, *Forward from Liberalism* (London: Gollancz, 1937), 174.

86. Malcolm Muggeridge, *The Thirties: 1930–1940 in Great Britain* (1940; London: Collins, 1967), 183.

87. Herbert Read, *The Contrary Experience* (London: Faber, 1963), 11.

88. Aldous Huxley, *On the Margin* (London: Chatto & Windus, 1923), 22–23.

89. Huxley, *On the Margin*, 23, 25.

90. Huxley, *Ends and Means*, 313–14.

91. Huxley, *Do What You Will*, 226.

92. Huxley, *Ends and Means*, 143.

93. Huxley, *Ends and Means*, 313, 317.

94. Huxley, *Ends and Means*, 313.

95. Aldous Huxley, "Progress: How the Achievements of Civilization Will Eventually Bankrupt the Entire World," *Vanity Fair*, January 1928, 69.

96. Huxley, "Progress," 105.

97. Thody, *Aldous Huxley: A Biographical Introduction*, 51.

98. Firchow, *End of Utopia*, 40.

99. Bertrand Russell, *The Scientific Outlook* (New York: W. W. Norton, 1931), 260.

100. Russell, *Scientific Outlook*, 100.

Notes

101. Russell, *Scientific Outlook*, 151–52.

102. Russell, *Scientific Outlook*, 175, 152.

103. Russell, *Scientific Outlook*, 208, 198.

104. Bertrand Russell, *The Practice and Theory of Bolshevism* (London: George Allen, 1920), 183.

105. See David Beetham, *Bureaucracy* (Minneapolis: University of Minnesota Press, 1987), 11–12.

106. Aldous Huxley, *Themes and Variations* (New York: Harper & Brothers, 1950), 58.

107. Quoted in Beetham, *Bureaucracy*, 61.

108. Russell, *Scientific Outlook*, 211–12.

109. Russell, *Scientific Outlook*, 224–25.

110. Russell, *Scientific Outlook*, 229, 234, 225, 248, 237.

111. Russell, *Scientific Outlook*, 261.

112. Russell, *Scientific Outlook*, 182–83.

113. Russell, *Scientific Outlook*, 236.

114. Russell, *Scientific Outlook*, 213–15.

115. Huxley, *Proper Studies*, 266.

116. Huxley, "Outlook for American Culture," 265.

117. Huxley, "Outlook for American Culture," 268, 270, 269, 270.

118. Huxley, *Proper Studies*, 281–82.

119. Aldous Huxley, "Whither Are We Civilizing?" *Vogue*, April 1928, 64.

120. Huxley, "Whither Are We Civilizing?" 124.

121. Huxley, *Proper Studies*, 136.

122. See Huxley's *Proper Studies*, especially page 24. Huxley also rejected the modern state as it was organized along democratic lines (including universal suffrage and education).

123. Huxley, *Proper Studies*, 159.

124. Michel Foucault, *Discipline and Punish: The Birth of the Prison*, trans. Alan Sheridan (New York: Vintage-Random House, 1979), 169.

125. See chapter 23 of Keith Sward's *The Legend of Henry Ford* (New York: Rinehart & Co., 1948). While some of these practices did not take place until after the publication of *Brave New World*, for the most part, they typify Ford worker supervision throughout the 1920s and 1930s.

126. See chapter 7 of Sward's *The Legend of Henry Ford*. Ford's remark on history is quoted on page 110.

127. Huxley, *Proper Studies*, 270.

128. Huxley, *Letters*, 351.

129. Huxley, *Music at Night,* 213–14.

130. Huxley, *Proper Studies,* 49.

131. Huxley, *Music at Night,* 212–13.

132. Huxley, *Music at Night,* 147.

133. Huxley, *Point Counter Point,* 415.

134. Huxley, *Music at Night,* 143–46.

135. Huxley, *Music at Night,* 149.

136. Firchow, *End of Utopia,* 73.

137. Huxley, "Whither Are We Civilizing?" 124.

138. Huxley, *Proper Studies,* 18–19.

139. Huxley, *Proper Studies,* 220.

140. Huxley, *Proper Studies,* 242.

Bibliography

Primary Sources

Fisher, H. A. L. *A History of Europe*. Vol. 3, *The Liberal Experiment*. New York: Houghton Mifflin, 1936.

Ford, Henry. *Moving Forward*. Garden City, N.Y.: Doubleday, Doran & Co., 1922.

———. *My Life and Work*. Garden City, N.Y.: Garden City Publishing Co., 1922.

———. *My Philosophy of Industry*. New York: Coward-McCann, 1929.

Huxley, Aldous. *After Many a Summer Dies the Swan*. London: Chatto & Windus, 1939.

———. *Antic Hay*. London: Chatto & Windus, 1923.

———. "Boundaries of Utopia," *Virginia Quarterly Review* 7 (January 1931): 47–54.

———. *Brave New World*. New York: Harper & Row, Publishers, 1932.

———. *Brave New World Revisited*. London: Chatto & Windus, 1959.

———. *Crome Yellow*. London: Chatto & Windus, 1921.

———. *Do What You Will*. London: Chatto & Windus, 1929.

———. *Eyeless in Gaza*. London: Chatto & Windus, 1936.

———. *Letters*, ed. Grover Smith. London: Chatto & Windus, 1969.

———. *Music at Night*. London: Chatto & Windus, 1931.

———. *The Olive Tree*. London: Chatto & Windus, 1936.

———. "The Outlook for American Culture: Some Reflections in a Machine Age," *Harper's Magazine* 155 (August 1927): 265–70.

———. *Point Counter Point*. London: Chatto & Windus, 1928.

———. "Progress: How the Achievements of Civilization Will Eventually Bankrupt the Entire World," *Vanity Fair* 29 (January 1928): 59–105.

———. *Proper Studies*. London: Chatto & Windus, 1927.

————. *Themes and Variations*. London: Chatto & Windus, 1950.

————. *Those Barren Leaves*. London: Chatto & Windus, 1925.

Orwell, George. *Nineteen Eighty-Four*. Oxford: Clarendon Press, 1984.

Russell, Bertrand. *Icarus*. London: Kegan Paul, 1924.

————. *The Scientific Outlook*. New York: W.W. Norton & Co., 1931.

————. *The Practice and Theory of Bolshevism*. London: George Allen & Unwin Ltd., 1920.

Wells, H. G. *The Works of H. G. Wells*. Vol. 28, *Men Like Gods*, New York: Scribners, 1927.

————. *The Works of H. G. Wells*. Vol. 2, *The Sleeper Awakes*. New York: Scribners, 1924.

Zamyatin, Yevgeny. *We*. New York: Avon Books, 1983.

Secondary Sources

Adorno, Theodor W. *Negative Dialectics*. New York: Continuum Publishing Company, 1987.

Aldridge, Alexandra. *The Scientific World View in Dystopia*. Ann Arbor: UMI Research Press, 1984.

Atkinson, R. F. *Knowledge and Explanation in History: An Introduction to the Philosophy of History*. Ithaca: Cornell University Press, 1978.

Baker, Robert S. *The Dark Historic Page: Social Satire and Historicism in the Novels of Aldous Huxley, 1921–1939*. Madison: University of Wisconsin Press, 1982.

Bedford, Sybille. *Aldous Huxley: A Biography*. New York: Alfred A. Knopf/ Harper and Row, 1974. The standard biography.

Beetham, David. *Bureaucracy*. Minneapolis: University of Minnesota Press, 1987.

Bleich, David. *Utopia: The Psychology of a Cultural Fantasy*. Ann Arbor: UMI Research Press, 1984.

Brander, Laurence. *Aldous Huxley: A Critical Study*. Lewisburg: Bucknell University Press, 1970. A general survey of Huxley's work.

Brown, E. J. *Brave New World, 1984, and We: An Essay on Anti-Utopia*. Ann Arbor: Ardis, 1976.

Carr, Edward Hallett. *The Twenty Years Crisis, 1919–1939*. London: Macmillan, 1954.

Collins, Christopher. *Evgenij Zamjatin: An Interpretive Study*. The Hague: Mouton, 1973. One of the most perceptive studies of Zamiatin.

Bibliography

Connors, James. "Zamiatin's *We* and the Genesis of 1984." *Modern Fiction* 21 (Spring 1975): 107–24.

Firchow, Peter Edgerly. *Aldous Huxley: Satirist and Novelist.* Minneapolis: University of Minnesota Press, 1972. A fine survey of Huxley's satirical technique.

———. *The End of Utopia: A Study of Aldous Huxley's Brave New World.* Lewisburg: Bucknell University Press, 1984. This is essential reading for the sources of Huxley's dystopia, a thorough and important study.

Ferns, C. S. *Aldous Huxley: Novelist.* London: Athlone Press, 1980. Some interesting ideas on popular responses to Huxley's novels but basically superficial plot summary. The chapter on *Brave New World* is shallow and unoriginal.

Foucault, Michel. *Discipline and Punish: The Birth of the Prison.* New York: Vintage, 1979.

Fourier, Charles. *Design for Utopia.* Ed. Charles Gide. New York: Schocken Books, 1971.

Fox, R. M. *The Triumphant Machine.* London: Hogarth, 1928.

Freud, Sigmund. *The Future of an Illusion.* Trans. James Strachey. New York: W. W. Norton, 1961.

———. *Works.* Trans. James Strachey. London: Hogarth, 1961.

Garrett, Garet. *Ouroborous, or the Mechanical Extension of Mankind.* London: Kegan Paul, 1925.

Haldane, Charlotte. *Man's World.* London: Chatto & Windus, 1926.

Haldane, J. B. S. "Biological Possibilities for the Human Species in the Next Ten Thousand Years." In *Man and His Future.* Ed. Gordon Wolstenholme. London: J. A. Churchill, 1963.

———. *Daedalus.* New York: Dutton, 1924.

———. *Science and Human Life.* New York: Harper, 1933.

Jameson, Fredric. *The Political Unconscious: Narrative as a Socially Symbolic Act.* Ithaca: Cornell University Press, 1981.

Jennings, H. S. *Prometheus, or Biology and the Advancement of Man.* London: Kegan Paul, 1926.

Kateb, George. *Utopia and Its Enemies.* Glencoe: Free Press, 1963.

Kemp, Peter. *H. G. Wells and the Culminating Ape.* New York: St. Martin's Press, 1982.

Keynes, John Maynard. *Essays in Biography.* New York: Harcourt, Brace and Company, 1933.

Lasch, Christopher. *The Minimal Self: Psychic Survival in Troubled Times.* New York: W. W. Norton, 1984.

Leach, Gerald. *The Biocrats.* London: Jonathan Cape, 1970.

Lytton, Edward Bulwer. *The Coming Race*. London: Oxford, 1928.

Mannheim, Karl. *Ideology and Utopia: An Introduction to the Sociology of Knowledge*. London: Routledge and Kegan Paul, 1966.

Mandelbaum, Maurice. *The Anatomy of Historical Knowledge*. Baltimore: Johns Hopkins University Press, 1977.

Manuel, F. E. and F. P. *Utopian Thought in the Western World*. Cambridge: Harvard University Press, 1979.

May, Keith. *Aldous Huxley*. New York: Barnes and Noble, 1972. An excellent survey of Huxley's work; chapter 5 offers a concise and provocative reading of *Brave New World*.

Mazlish, Bruce. *The Riddle of History: The Great Speculators from Vico to Freud*. New York: Harper and Row, 1955.

McLellan, David. *Ideology*. Minneapolis: University of Minnesota Press, 1986.

Meckier, Jerome. *Aldous Huxley: Satire and Structure*. London: Chatto and Windus, 1969. A thorough and penetrating study of Huxley's works; chapter 7 focuses on *Brave New World* as well as Huxley's other utopian writings.

———. "A Neglected Huxley 'Preface': His Earliest Synopsis of *Brave New World*." *Twentieth Century Literature* 25 (Spring 1979): 1–20.

———. "Our Ford, Our Freud and the Behaviourist Conspiracy in Huxley's *Brave New World*." *Thalia* 1 (1977–78): 35–39. An important assessment of Huxley's use of psychology in *Brave New World*.

Moody, C. "Zamiatin's *We* and English Antiutopian Fiction." *UNISA English Studies* 14 (1976): 24–33.

Mowat, Charles Loch. *Britain Between the Wars, 1918–1940*. Chicago: University of Chicago Press, 1955.

Muggeridge, Malcolm. *The Thirties: 1930–1940 in Great Britain*. London: Collins, 1940.

Muller, H. J. *Out of the Night, A Biologist's View of the Future*. London: Gollancz, 1936.

Needham, Joseph. *Man a Machine*. London: Kegan Paul, 1927.

Nisbet, Robert. *History of the Idea of Progress*. New York: Basic Books, 1980.

Schmalhausen, S. D., ed. *Behold America!* New York: Farrar and Rinehart, 1931.

Shane, Alex M. *The Life and Works of Evgenij Zamjatin*. Berkeley: University of California Press, 1968.

Shklar, Judith N. *After Utopia*. Princeton, N.J.: Princeton University Press, 1957.

Bibliography

Siegfried, André. *America Comes of Age.* New York: Harcourt, Brace and Co., 1928.

Snow, Melinda. "The Gray Parody in *Brave New World.*" *Papers on Language and Literature* 13 (Winter 1977): 85–88.

Spender, Stephen. *The Destructive Element: A Study of Modern Writers and Beliefs.* London: Jonathan Cape, 1935.

Sward, Keith. *The Legend of Henry Ford.* New York: Rinehart and Company, 1948.

Taylor, A. J. P. *English History, 1914–1945.* London: Oxford University Press, 1955.

Taylor, Frederick Winslow. *The Principles of Scientific Management.* New York: W. W. Norton, 1967.

Thody, Philip. *Aldous Huxley: A Biographical Introduction.* New York: Charles Scribner's Sons, 1973. A brief but very insightful study; chapter 4 is a concise, interesting reading of *Brave New World.*

Thompson, David. *Europe Since Napoleon.* New York: Alfred A. Knopf, 1971.

Watson, J. B. and William McDougall. *The Battle of Behaviorism.* London: Kegan Paul, 1928.

Watt, Donald, ed. *Aldous Huxley: The Critical Heritage.* London: Routledge and Kegan Paul, 1975. An essential volume containing a wide range of reviews of all of Huxley's books, including Orwell's assessment of Huxley's antiutopia. Watt's introduction is a useful overview of Huxley's career.

Watt, Donald. "The Manuscript Revisions of *Brave New World.*" *Journal of English and German Philology* 77 (July 1978): 367–82.

Watts, Harold. *Aldous Huxley.* New York: Twayne, 1959. An interesting biographical-critical study.

White, Hayden. *Metahistory: The Historical Imagination in Nineteenth-Century Europe.* Baltimore: Johns Hopkins University Press, 1973.

Woodcock, George. *The Crystal Spirit: A Study of George Orwell.* Boston: Little, Brown and Co., 1966.

———. *Dawn and the Darkest Hour: A Study of Aldous Huxley.* New York: Viking, 1972. A valuable study by one of Huxley's contemporaries. Chapter 7 contains a brief but interesting discussion of *Brave New World.*

Index

Index

About the Author

Robert S. Baker is Professor of English at the University of Wisconsin at Madison. He received his B.A. and M.A. from the University of Western Ontario and his Ph.D. from the University of Illinois. He is the author of *The Dark Historic Page: Social Satire and Historicism in the Novels of Aldous Huxley, 1921–1939* and has published criticism on Charles Dickens, George Meredith, Henry James, and Patrick White. His area of specialization is nineteenth- and twentieth-century British literature. In 1981, he received the Chancellor's Award for Excellence in Teaching at the University of Wisconsin.